CAN INTELLIGENT PEOPLE BELIEVE?

CAN INTELLIGENT PEOPLE BELIEVE?

by

Tom Rees

HODDER AND STOUGHTON

LONDON SYDNEY AUCKLAND TORONTO

CONTENTS

PREFACE

This book consists of a collection of sermons by Tom
Rees, that prince of evangelists. I don't know how many
times he preached them, because he was not averse to
using the same material dozens of times over (and every
time with compelling freshness!), but as far as I know
they were first used in their present form and with their
present title in a series of Saturday evening youth
rallies in the City Temple in the winter of 1962. At that
time I was vicar of two country parishes in Essex, and
we managed to rustle up a coachload of young people to
go to the first of the series.

What a memorable evening! The young people from
our villages had never seen anything like it in their
lives: hundreds of cheerful people in a London church
singing and laughing their hearts out. And after having to cope with twenty minutes of me on a Sunday
evening they couldn't get over the length of the sermon:
'Fifty-five minutes, and it seemed like fifteen,' they said,
amazed at themselves as much as at the preacher. I felt
duly crushed; but what was that, compared with the
knowledge that some of them had found a new faith in
Christ that night.

I have sat under Tom Rees' preaching for over twenty
years, and have now been relishing him again in this
printed form. Though he was always his own inimitable
self in the pulpit or on the platform, his style of preaching changed a lot over the years. He used jocularly to
say that if ever an evangelist backslid, he became a Bible-
teacher, and it is a fact that Tom's preaching became

more biblical and more meaty as he grew older. But he
never lost his evangelistic gift. Basic teaching sermons on
doctrinal subjects would turn, effortlessly and naturally,
into evangelistic appeals, because Tom Rees knew that
as he could depend less and less on his hearers having
some knowledge of Christian truth he had to supply
more scriptural content in his teaching before ever he
could press for commitment.

   These chapters must then be read as sermons. Read
them with imagination, and if you ever heard Tom
preach, *listen* to his words and the gripping way he
spoke them as you read these pages. Hear the inflections
of his voice, the variations of pitch, the dramatic pauses,
the flashes of humour. It is not the froth and bubble of
the instant-conversion, 'come to Jesus' preacher. This is
a man's man talking to men's minds and showing them
the reasonableness and the compulsion of Christian
commitment. Tom Rees' aim was absolutely clear and
transparent. He never concealed the purpose of his meetings: it was frankly to bring his hearers to Christ. He
did this with a degree of passionate sincerity that I
have found in no one else, and he proved his genuine-
ness by the amount he prayed. He knew that success in
evangelism comes only through prayer, and so he prayed.
Many Christian activities believe in prayer but leave
little time for it. They rely on others to pray for them,
while they do the work. Tom really did pray himself—
often by the hour. That is why the conversions followed.

   So, in his absence, I ask you to pray that his words now
committed to print will do more than inspire nostalgic
recollections of the past but lead many to a new trust in
Jesus Christ as their Saviour and Lord.

                                      JOHN B. TAYLOR

      Vice-Principal,
        Oak Hill College,
         London, N14

CHAPTER ONE

THE VIRGIN BIRTH

If we are going to understand what the New Testament has to say about the virgin birth of Jesus of Nazareth, we should understand what the Jewish customs were in the time of Christ concerning couples being engaged, betrothed and married. It was very different from the days in which we live. First there was the engagement, which often took place when the couple were children. The father and mother usually fixed it up with some other father and mother, or if they could not do it, they sometimes employed a professional match-maker. Very often the young couple never met or saw one another. Sometimes they did not even know the name of the other person. However, when the young couple were mature, usually in their early twenties, they took the second step, referred to in Luke and again in Matthew, which is known in the Jewish world as the betrothal. At the time of the betrothal the girl could, if she wished, say that she did not wish to proceed further. The betrothal lasted usually twelve months. When the couple were betrothed, they were called husband and wife. The girl did not refer to her engaged husband as her fiancé but as her husband.

He talked about her as his wife. Matthew refers to the fact that Mary is the wife of Joseph, when in fact she was not actually his wife as we know it. During the betrothal period the man continued to live in his home with his people, while the girl lived in her home with her people, and in normal circumstances they did not meet unless they were chaperoned. That did not mean that they never had time to talk together, or to hold hands and do things that young people do, always have done and always will do! But it did mean that they were chaperoned. The betrothal could only be broken by what they referred to as a divorce. Once they were betrothed, they belonged to one another. Only death or divorce could part them. And practically the only cause for divorce that was known at that time was unfaithfulness. If, for instance, the girl was found to be pregnant, and her espoused husband was not responsible, then immediately, as the injured party, he would go to the council, the local synagogue possibly, and he would tell them what had happened. A trial would be arranged. The presiding priest would be the judge, and according to the Law of Moses, which was the law that Joseph and Mary with their strong Jewish background knew and recognised, unfaithfulness of that sort was punishable by death. There are serious passages in the Old Testament concerning such events. If the espoused wife was found unfaithful, and proved guilty, then the injured espoused husband was to take the first stone and cast it at her, and she was to be stoned until she died. The one who committed sin with her was also to be put to death without mercy.

God takes an extremely serious view of unfaithfulness, of fornication or adultery. Joseph and Mary of Nazareth also took an extremely serious view of unfaithfulness. Their standards of behaviour and morality were probably above anything that we know and understand today. At the end of the betrothal the marriage proper took place, and from the marriage proper the betrothed husband and the betrothed wife lived together and enjoyed the privileges of husband and wife as we know them after a marriage in this country.

Joseph and Mary were not married in the sense that we know it. They were only betrothed, which to us means engaged, only engaged in a way that was binding, engaged in a way that could not be broken except by death or divorce. It was during this twelve-month period that the events which we are considering took place.

Moreover, Joseph was not an old man with a bent back, and grey hair, doddering around, and Mary was not an old bent woman, dressed as a nun. They were a perfectly normal, healthy, happy young couple, full of life and fun, full of happiness, yet truly committed to God. God-fearing people. How do we know? Well, Matthew tells us that Joseph was a just man, which means he was a law-abiding man, and as for Mary, she was steeped in the Scriptures. Her song, a most beautiful piece of poetry, which we know as the Magnificat, is a whole string of lovely Scriptures, some thirty-three of them, collected from the Old Testament. Her heart and mind must have been stored with the Word of God. I do not suppose for a moment that she had ever heard of my book about learning the Bible by heart, but she knew

what it was to learn the Bible by heart. More than likely
she knew all the Psalms and most of the Prophets. The
young people did. All the angel had to do was to quote
some minor prophet, and Joseph understood immediately. So we are not dealing with a young couple who
were irreligious. They were intensely religious, with high
moral standards, and a great fear of God, with reverence
for His holy Law and love for His most holy Word.

I do not know how long they had been 'going steady',
but they lived in the same town. They were normal
young people, and undoubtedly when they went to the
synagogue their eyes would meet Sabbath by Sabbath.
And unless I am gravely mistaken, they would find some
way of getting together afterwards and talking. They
would be making plans for the marriage. They were betrothed, everyone knew. Probably in the evenings she
would go round to the carpenter's shop, where I imagine
he was working late building furniture for their home,
and she would help. Oh yes, they had plans together.
You think they discussed a family? I think it is more
than likely. Young folk who are approaching marriage
usually do. Yet they did everything in the fear of the
Lord. How they loved one another, in the true sense of
the word, so deeply and so truly. Then one day, quite
unexpectedly, Mary had a vision. The angel Gabriel, who
stands in the presence of God, appeared unto her, and
addressed her in odd, frightening language. 'Hail, thou
that art highly favoured, the Lord is with thee; blessed
art thou among women.' And when she saw him she was
troubled, as well she might be, and she cast in her mind
what manner of salutation this could be. One is not sur-

prised that this sensitive, beautiful girl was frightened. And then Gabriel, speaking with all the tenderness of heaven, said, 'Fear not, Mary. Fear not, for thou hast found favour with God. Mary, thou shalt conceive in thy womb, and bring forth a son. He shall be great. Thou shalt call His name Jesus. He shall reign over the house of Jacob for ever.'

Mary was profoundly disturbed. She was no ignorant child. Looking into the face of the angel, she asked, 'How shall this be (how can I, a virgin, conceive in my womb and bring forth a son) seeing that I know not a man? (I have had no intercourse with any man)?' The angel answered, 'The Holy Ghost shall come upon thee, and the power of the Highest shall overshadow thee, therefore also that holy thing which shall be born of thee shall be called the son of ... Joseph? ... No, the Son of God.'

'Behold, the handmaid of the Lord. Be it unto me according to thy word.'

It is not strictly correct to say that Jesus of Nazareth had a supernatural birth. On the contrary, it is strictly correct to say that Jesus of Nazareth had a natural birth. He was born as you were born, as I was born. He had a natural birth, but He had a supernatural conception. The Apostles' Creed puts it very simply and very beautifully. 'He (our Lord Jesus Christ) was conceived by the Holy Ghost, He was born of the Virgin Mary.' 'How shall this be?' asked Mary. 'The Holy Ghost shall come upon thee, the power of the Highest shall overshadow thee, therefore that holy thing that shall be born of thee shall be called the Son of God.' The angel added this important piece of information, which helped Mary to solve her problem. 'And, behold,' said the angel, 'thy cousin, Elisabeth, she also hath conceived a son in her old age; and this is the sixth month with her who was called barren. With God,' said the angel, 'nothing is impossible.'

What was Mary's immediate reaction? Did she rush to Joseph and tell him? She dared not. I do not think she even told her own mother. She arose with haste, and went seventy miles south to Elisabeth. As she went there was one big question in her heart and in her mind. Was it a dream, or was it true? Was it a figment of imagination, or did God speak? Only twenty more miles to go, and then I shall know. If my elderly cousin is pregnant with child, then I shall know. If she is not pregnant, then it was a dream. My doubts and my torture will be gone.

When she entered into the house of Zachariah, her cousin Elisabeth was full of the Holy Ghost, and spake out with a loud voice, 'Blessed art thou among women, and blessed is the fruit of thy womb. What is this to me that the mother of my Lord should come to me?' And then, filled with the joy of heaven, unable to speak in human language, this wonderful girl, this pure Hebrew virgin, lifted up her heart. 'My soul doth magnify the Lord, and my spirit hath rejoiced in God my Saviour. For He hath regarded the low estate of His handmaiden; for behold, from henceforth all generations shall call me blessed. For He that is mighty hath done to me great things, and holy is His name. And His mercy is on them that fear Him from generation to generation.' She stayed with her cousin Elisabeth until a week or so before John the Baptist was born, then she returned, knowing that she was with child. Wondering, filled with doubts and forebodings and problems. Would her beloved Joseph believe her story, or would he think that . . .? He was not the father of her unborn child, that was evident. If he did not believe her story of the angel, and the coming of the Holy Spirit upon her, it meant disgrace, divorce, a trial, possibly death.

I do not know what she said. I do not know how she broke it to him, but Matthew makes it clear that her worst fears were realised. Joseph did not believe her. He could not believe. This talk of Gabriel coming and speaking to his betrothed wife. Matthew says, 'Now the birth of Jesus Christ was on this wise. When as His mother Mary was espoused to Joseph before they came together, she was found with child of the Holy Spirit. Then Joseph, her husband (but he's her espoused husband, not actual husband) being a just man (who feared God), and not willing to make her a public example, was minded to put her away privily (breaking off the engagement, divorcing her quietly).'

Joseph was facing a tremendous issue. He was a convinced and devout Jew, and he was committed to the Law, and the Law said that if during the time of an espousal a partner was found and proved to be unfaithful—and what could it mean when she was found with child but that she had been unfaithful?—she must go to the council, and the elders, and he must accuse her of adultery. And they must bring her out publicly, and she must be tried and humiliated and judged, and if she was found guilty, she must be condemned. The Law said, 'Joseph, you must do it.' Joseph was a just man, and his sense of justice and his loyalty to the Law said, 'Joseph, try her, judge her, punish her, condemn her. You must if you are going to fear God.' It was not quite so simple as that. This couple loved one another. Then Joseph hardened.

When he finished work he knocked the sawdust from his tunic and went over the hillside, and he prayed under the starlit heaven. He wrestled with this problem. How could he spare his loved one the humiliation of it all? But how could he forgive her? He was not willing to make her a public example. His mind and his conscience said, 'Condemn her and judge her, punish her. You must.' But his heart said, 'No, forgive her, be compassionate and merciful.' What was he to do?

I do not know whether they met during this time. I have a feeling that Mary hid herself away, and would not see him. Then her prayers were answered. 'And,' says Matthew, 'while he considered these things, behold, the angel of the Lord appeared unto him in a dream.' What a busy time Gabriel had going backwards and forwards! He had to go down and explain it all to Zachariah, and then he had to explain it to Mary, and now he's back again on the same task to explain it to Joseph. But who would not enjoy preaching good news about a coming Saviour?

'Joseph, thou son of David'—he gave him his correct title—'Joseph,' said the angel. 'Fear not to take unto thee Mary thy wife.' Fear not to proceed with the marriage ceremony. Fear not to get married properly. There is no reason why you should not. 'Fear not . . . for that which is conceived in her is of the Holy Ghost. And she

shall bring forth a son, and thou shalt call His name
Jesus (God our Saviour) for He shall deliver His people
from their sins.' The angel went on, 'All this will happen, a virgin shall conceive, a virgin shall bring forth a
child that it might be fulfilled which is written by the
prophets.' And then he quoted Isaiah's words from the
seventh chapter and the fourteenth verse. 'Behold, a virgin shall be with child, and shall bring forth a son, and
they shall call His name Emmanuel.' What does it
mean? God with us. It was enough for Joseph. Joseph
believed in the Hebrew prophets. 'Then Joseph,' says
Matthew, 'being raised from sleep, did as the angel of
the Lord had bidden him.' He proceeded with the marriage arrangements, and he took unto him his wife.
Matthew says, 'He knew her not'—the marriage was not
consummated—'until she had brought forth her first-
born son. And they called his name Jesus.'

As the prophet foretold, the Messiah was born of a
virgin. But another prophet, Micah, had foretold that
He would not be born in Nazareth in the north, but in
Bethlehem, in the province of Judaea. What was God
going to do about this? The young couple, Mary with
child, lived seventy miles—three days' journey—away
from the little village of Bethlehem. God put it into the
heart of Caesar Augustus that all the world should be
taxed. One day this couple met with joy and delight, and
I can almost hear Joseph saying, 'Mary, our problem is
solved. There will be no questions asked about the baby
born early during our marriage. No questions at all. I've
got to go, I've got to travel seventy miles back to my
home. You know, of course, that I'm descended from the

royal house of David. I've got to go back again to Bethlehem of Judaea, and you're coming with me.' What
could be nicer than a honeymoon trip down to the big
city? They set out, leaving a good deal earlier than they
need, and they went to visit Elisabeth, and see the new-
born John the Baptist.

On the night of the census, they arrived in Bethlehem
of Judaea, the very place where the prophet said the
Messiah was to be born: 'And thou, Bethlehem, in the
land of Juda, are not least among the princes of Juda,
for out of thee shall come a Governor, and He shall rule
my people Israel.' There was no room for them in the
inn, so they had to spend the night in the stable. And
that night the cattle heard a baby cry, and angels sang
in heaven.

Luke tells us concerning these events that 'Mary the
mother of Jesus, kept all these things, and pondered
them in her heart'. She did not discuss them with everyone. They probably would not have believed her anyhow.
She discussed it with Joseph. He understood. She discussed it, no doubt, with Elisabeth, and with Elisabeth's
husband, Zacharias. I think that apart from that little
group no one else knew. When our Lord began His public ministry, I am certain that the Jews knew nothing
about it. I am certain too that the disciples knew nothing
about it. And it helps in reading the four Gospels to bear
in mind that the people were ignorant of these two facts
—that Jesus was conceived of the Holy Ghost, born of
the Virgin Mary, and that Jesus was born in Bethlehem
of Judaea. They thought He was born in Nazareth, in
Galilee. Mary kept all these things, and pondered them

in her heart.

When our Lord was twelve years of age, they visited Jerusalem. He stayed behind in the temple, but they, supposing him to be with the company, returned north again. They went up every year for the feast. It was a great annual pilgrimage. After three days they found Him back in Jerusalem sitting in the temple. Mary made a blunder. Naturally, she always referred to Joseph as 'your father' when she spoke to Jesus, because he was His stepfather, the legal father, Jesus was born in wedlock, and all the neighbours supposed that Joseph was the father of Jesus. Therefore when she found Him, she said this to Him. Listen to the first recorded words of Jesus as a child of twelve. Said Mary, 'Why hast thou dealt thus with us? Thy father and I have sought thee sorrowing.' Back came a rebuke. 'Wist ye not that I must be about my Father's business?' Even then, says Luke, Mary kept these words and pondered them in her heart. He was crucified because He, Jesus of Nazareth, said—not once, not twice, but again and again—that God was His own particular Father, He was God's own Son, in a unique way. When the people heard Him say that, they said, 'Blasphemy! We have a law, and by our law he ought to die, for he being a man maketh himself God. The Son of God, indeed! Is not this the son of Joseph? His father and mother we know. How is it then that he saith, "I came down from heaven?" What's all this?'

Because Jesus said that He was God's own particular Son they condemned Him to death on a charge of blasphemy. Because of that they nailed Him to the

Cross. It is evident that Joseph died before this happened. There is a touching scene in John's account of the crucifixion. While Jesus hung there in agony and bloody sweat, there stood by the Cross, Mary his mother. Did she then understand what the aged Simeon had said when she went to present the child Jesus, 'Yea, and a sword shall pierce through thy own soul also'? I think she did. If Jesus of Nazareth was not conceived by the Holy Ghost and born of the Virgin Mary—if that was not so—why did not Mary step forth during the trial or during the crucifixion and save her son from that agony and the shame of the Cross? She needed only to say, 'I know the father of that man. I am the guilty woman. He is no son of God. This story of God being his own particular Father, and he being God's own particular Son, is a lie. I know the name of his father. I married that man.' She never said a word. Why not? Because she knew that the one hanging there in front of a jeering mob, the naked child that she had seen years ago in the stable of Bethlehem, surrounded by the dung of animals, she knew that He was the Saviour. She knew that on the Cross God was in Christ, suffering, bleeding and dying for the sin of the world, for your sin and my sin. That is why He came into the world. Most babies are born that they might live. He was born that He might die. For you.

CHAPTER TWO

THE BIBLE

Can an intelligent person believe in the Bible? Read the
words of our Lord in the fifth chapter of St. John's
Gospel, 'The Father Himself which hath sent me, hath
borne witness of me.' 'Search the Scriptures . . . they are
they which testify of me.' 'Had ye believed Moses, ye
would have believed me, for Moses wrote of me. But if ye
believe not Moses or the words of Moses, how can ye
believe me?'

If you want to convey your thoughts or ideas to any-
body, the normal way to do it is by using a word, or
words, as the case may be. If the person is near to you,
you will talk to them. It is the spoken word, and through
your words you express yourself. If the person is away,
you will get paper, ink and pen, and you will write.
Through the spoken word or the written word you convey your thoughts or ideas. You also convey yourselves.
We get to know each other mainly through words.

God has expressed Himself—He has made Himself
known to us—in Jesus Christ, His Son and our Lord.
Therefore John refers to Jesus as the Word of God. 'In
the beginning was the Word, and the Word was with

God, and the Word was God.' Our Lord is referred to as
'the living Word of God'. As I get to know you through
your words, so I come to know God the Father through
the living Word, Jesus Christ. To see Jesus is to see the
Father, to hear Jesus is to hear the Father, to watch
Jesus at work is to witness the Father at work, to know
Jesus is to know the Father. That is why He came as the
Word of God, as the chosen, real essence of God. 'Well,'
you say, 'that's all very well. I can understand how Peter,
James, John and Thomas and the rest got to know God
in and through Jesus, because they heard Him talk, they
looked into His face, they watched Him, but unfortun-
ately for us He lived and died two thousand years ago.'
There is no need for us to remain in the darkness. God
has not only revealed Himself, first and foremost in His
Son Jesus Christ our Lord, the living Word, He has also
revealed Himself in His written Word. And the living
Word of God, Jesus Christ, and the written Word of
God, the Bible, are very closely allied. That is why Jesus
says, 'The Father Himself hath borne witness of me.'
'The Scriptures . . . they testify of me.' 'But if ye believe
not Moses' writings, how can ye believe my words?'
Those who reject the written Word invariably reject the
living Word. Or to put it differently, I have noticed that
those who really love Jesus Christ are those who really
love the Bible and believe in it and get to know it. One
of the surest ways of judging a person's love and devo-
tion for our Lord, the living Word, is through their at-
titude towards the Bible, God's written Word.

I have not always believed, as I now believe, that the
Bible is God's Word to man. I was not brought up to be-

lieve in the Bible and to believe in Jesus Christ. I was told authoritatively that the Bible was a good book, but there were other good books too. I was told that the Bible contained truth, but also that it contained error, and nobody quite knew what was reliable and what was not reliable. I was told that Jesus was a good man—in fact, that He was not only a good man but He was the very best of men, the most holy man that ever walked the earth. But He was no more, I was told, than a good man. I was told that no scientist or doctor believed in the virgin birth; that, of course, was pure fiction. And although we must respect Jesus of Nazareth and meditate upon His words, we must go no further. The result of that teaching in my home, my church and my school was—I think myself that it was the inevitable result—I became a complete agnostic. Not an atheist. An atheist has got a creed. Here it is, 'There is no God.' He is very emphatic about it. I was an agnostic. Another word for agnostic is ignoramus—exactly the same word, they both mean the same, one Greek, the other Latin. So if you are an agnostic, do not boast about it, because you are boasting about being an ignorant person. An agnostic is a person who does not know. If you had asked me if I believed in God, I would have said, 'I don't know,' and I might have added, 'I don't care.' The vast majority of agnostics not only do not know but they do not care. God can forgive our ignorance, but it must be very hard to forgive our indifference.

If you have honest doubts about the existence of God, about the existence of Jesus Christ and about the truth of the Bible, you are not in the minority. The majority of people—thoughtful people—have doubts. Yes, and many of them are Christians too. So do not slink away into a corner with a guilty feeling that you alone have doubts. Doubts are common. It is a good thing to drag them to the light and discuss them with someone. And it is a good thing to meet together in a church study group, to thrash out why we believe what we believe. Through the prayers of my brother, the Rev. Dick Rees, I put my trust in Christ. And ever since I have been reading and re-reading this wonderful Book. I do not know how many times I have read it through, in many versions. I have also learned many of the books of the Bible by heart.

From being a disbeliever in the Bible, I have moved until I am convinced—I don't think or venture to suggest, but I am convinced—that this is God's Word to man. And through this Holy Book you, however deep your doubts, can come to know God. Not about Him—certainly that—but you can come to know Him in and through Jesus Christ, in a personal way. Jesus said, '*Ye*, search the Scriptures, for they are they which testify—which tell you about me.'

A couple of undergraduates were standing in one of the quads in Oxford. One was a Christian. In his hand he held a Bible, having come from church. The other man looked at him and said, 'What have you got there?' 'Oh,' he said, 'it's my Bible.' 'What do you carry that around for?' 'It means a lot to me, and helps me.' 'What,' he said, 'you don't believe that rubbish. That's just the same as any other book.' 'I know it isn't,' said the Christian. 'Well, I bet you can't prove to me that it's different from any other book.' 'I can,' said the Christian. 'I'll prove it to you. Please take my Bible and put it under your arm and walk three times around the quad. Will you do that?' 'Oh no, no . . .'

This is no ordinary book. It is a complete library of books, sixty-six of them in all, from Genesis in the Old Testament, running through to the Book of Revelation in the New Testament. The sixty-six books were not written by one man. They were not written either by a committee sitting round a table comparing notes. Scholars tell us that at least thirty-five different men wrote the sixty-six books of the Bible. They did not all live in the same country, and they did not all write in the same language. The Bible was written for the most part in Hebrew, Greek and Aramaic. The men who wrote were very different. Some were powerful and wealthy, and others were prisoners, having suffered the loss of all things, being in prison for writing the very truths, or preaching the very truths that they were writing. Some were brilliant, some were comparatively simple men. And there is one other thing that made it rather difficult for them to meet round a committee table—they did not all live at the same time. It took at least one thousand five hundred years for these thirty-five different men to write the sixty-six books of the Bible! Possibly the first book was the Book of Job, and more than likely the last one to be completed was the Gospel according to St. John.

Now you would imagine that having collected together sixty-six books written by thirty-five men over that vast period of time, living in different countries, speaking different languages, with very different backgrounds, you would have a conglomeration of religious notions and ideas contradicting one another. But the fascinating thing about the sixty-six books of the Bible is that although to the casual, shallow reader there may appear to be contradictions or inconsistencies, those who read and study and meditate, find there exists an amazing harmony. Rather than the books of the Bible contradicting one another they supplement each other. The people who talk the loudest about the inconsistencies and contradictions are invariably the people who know least about the Bible.

A man came to me after a meeting and said, 'Mr. Rees, you don't believe the Bible?' I said, 'Indeed I do.' 'Well,' he said, 'it's full of contradictions.' 'Oh, that's interesting. I've been reading it for many years, and I don't see the contradictions that you talk about.' 'But,' he said, 'the Bible's full of them.' 'Well,' I said, 'will you just show me one, please?' He took my Bible as if it was a hot brick. 'Well,' he said. 'It's somewhere . . . in one of the Gospels, I think . . .' 'If you don't mind,' I said, 'you'll save a lot of time if you look for the Gospels in the New Testament, not the Old!'

God forbid that I should say that the Bible is an easy book. You should not get the impression that it has no problems and no difficulties. If I should sit down and read my Bible from Genesis to Revelation and understand it and follow it, and put it back on my bookshelf and say, 'The Bible's fine. I've read it. Where's my next book?', then I would say to myself, 'The Bible is a human book, written by men with minds like mine.'

But I can read it and re-read it and study it and meditate upon it year after year, and the more I do it, the more I realise my utter ignorance of the Bible. As I meditate I see things that are not contrary to my understanding, but which again and again are beyond my understanding. I say to myself, 'This is no human book. It is God's Book.'

It has been my privilege to talk with scholars, who have told me that the more they read the more impressed they are with the harmony existing between the sixty-six books. How do you account for the harmony? Coincidence is ruled out. Supposing in London we decided to build a Commonwealth Building, and to make it novel, so that it was truly 'Commonwealth', we decided that it would be built of stones taken from quarries all over the Commonwealth. The ships come into the Port of London, and they start unloading great blocks of granite, or whatever the particular stone might be. They come shaped, all ready cut, from Canada, Australia, New Zealand, Africa—everywhere. The amazing thing is that each particular block fits perfectly into the next one. They do not have to do any chipping or make any alterations. It all fits into place. What do we say? Well, if we are fools, we stand back and claim, 'Well, of course, that's a remarkable coincidence that all those masons all over the world should each do what he thought he'd do and cut his chunk, and here it all fits. What a fluke!' If we were fools we would talk like that, but you would say, 'There's nothing remarkable about that, it's what I'd expect. Somewhere behind this building is the architect. He hands out the exact measurements and plans of every detail. I'd be surprised if these stones didn't fit.'

I only know one way of accounting for the harmony existing between the sixty-six books of the Bible, and that is by accepting the claim that the Bible makes for itself. This is what the Bible says: 'All Scripture is given by inspiration of·God.' Holy men, these thirty-five men of whom we have been speaking, they spake and they wrote, says the Bible, as they were moved, as they were carried along by the Holy Spirit. Although we have sixty-six books written by thirty-five different men, one thing is clear to every thoughtful person who reads—these thirty-five men were all inspired by the same Holy Spirit.

Right in the middle of the Bible, when the Old Testament had been completed, before the New Testament was started at all, our Lord Jesus Christ, the living Word of God, was born. He spoke, He suffered, He died, He rose from the dead. Looking back over the Old Testament Scriptures, Jesus said, 'The Scriptures . . . they bear witness (they testify) of me.' After His resurrection, on the Jerusalem to Emmaus road He walked along with Cleopas and his wife, and Luke tells us that beginning at Moses, Jesus expounded to them in all the Scriptures the things concerning Himself. 'Moses wrote of me,' said Jesus. Looking into the future, our Lord said, 'When the Holy Spirit is come, He will bring all things to your remembrance, whatsoever I have said unto you.' Matthew, Mark, Luke and John, writing under the guidance of the Holy Spirit, wrote in the four Gospels the things that Jesus had said to them. Jesus went on,

'I have yet many things to say to you, but you cannot
bear them now, howbeit when He the Spirit of truth is
come, He will guide you into all the truth.' And the
apostles, writing their letters, the Epistles, were taught
and guided by the Holy Spirit to explain and open up,
in the Epistles, the wonderful things that Jesus wanted
to say, but could not say to His disciples when He was
here on earth. The third thing Jesus said about the coming Spirit was this, 'When He is come, He will show you
things to come.' The apostle John, on the island of Pat-
mos, in the Spirit saw things to come. So we have the
three sections of the New Testament—the Gospels, the
Epistles, and the Book of Revelation. And in the Old
Testament—Moses, the Psalms and the Prophets. And
in the midst of the Old and New, our Lord and Saviour,
Jesus Christ. What did He say? Search, look, seek, work
it out, 'Search the Scriptures, for they are they which
bear witness of me.' 'The Father Himself hath borne
witness of me.' 'In the Scriptures ye have eternal life . . .
these are they which are able to make you wise unto
salvation through faith in me.' 'Moses wrote of me,'
said Jesus. 'He wrote of *me*.'

I am impressed not only by the harmony existing
between the books, but by the influence and the power
of this Holy Book, the Bible. In the year 1787 one of
His Majesty's transport ships sailed from Spithead. Captain Bligh was the captain, and the ship was the *Bounty*.
On board were between twenty and thirty sailors. Captain Bligh was pretty rough on them. He was a very
strict disciplinarian. They sailed for the South Seas to
collect bread-fruit trees, but when they landed at Tahiti,

they found a veritable paradise. Not only did they find
wonderful blue seas and golden sands, but they found
the most glamorous girls that sailors ever dreamed about.
Soon every sailor had his girlfriend, and to their great delight they stayed there several months. When Captain
Bligh eventually announced that the next day they were
setting sail, he was not very popular. Fletcher Christian
started mumbling and complaining and talking secretly
to some of the men about mutiny and staying there at
Tahiti for the rest of their lives, and getting rid of Captain Bligh and the *Bounty*. However, they sailed, but a
few days out, old Captain Bligh wakened one morning
and found himself looking into the barrel of a gun.
Fletcher Christian had organised a mutiny, and Captain
Bligh, with eighteen loyal members of the crew, were
put into the ship's long-boat and set drifting in the South
Sea Islands. Fletcher Christian and the eight mutineers
on board headed their ship back to Tahiti. When they
got back, without difficulty they persuaded not eight
but twelve girls to go on board with them, and they
headed back to sea. They had no plans, but after sailing
for some time, frightened in case they would be over-
taken, they came across Pitcairn Island—an extinct
volcano and a veritable paradise. There were no sands,
but steep cliffs, and luscious vegetation. They went
ashore and found no one living there, so they moved
everything they could from on board and set fire to the
Bounty, and watched her sink beneath the waves. Then
they turned round for 'paradise on earth', but actually
it was ten years of hell that they faced. One of the men
with the old copper kettle from the *Bounty*, rigged up a

distillery, and they distilled the roots of the trees, and started to make spirits. Before long the sailors and the women were incapable. They lived that way for days, weeks, months on end. Some of the men went mad and became like beasts. One flung himself over the cliff. They fought among themselves. After several years, there were only two men left, Edward Young and Alexander Smith. Young was an older man, ill with asthma. The women, with the eighteen children that had been born to them, one night seized the firearms and barricaded themselves in. The two remaining sailors lived alone. Neither the children nor the women would go near them. Young knew that he was dying. One day he went to the ship's chest, and at the bottom among the papers he found a book—old, bound in leather, somewhat mildewed and worm-eaten. He lifted it out. He had not read for years. The book he held in his hand was the *Bounty*'s Bible. He began at Genesis, chapter I. His friend Lex could not read a word, so he taught him to read. The two men, frightened and disillusioned, utter wrecks, together read the Bible. They read through Genesis, Exodus, Leviticus, Numbers, and as they read the fear of God came on them, and they both knew that God was holy and they were sinful. They did their best to pray. They read on, seeking for help and light, in the Old Testament. The little children were the first to come back, because they noticed the change in the men. The children brought the women back, and they used to sit down and listen while Edward Young and sometimes Smith, the younger man, spelt out the words to them. When they came to the Psalms they realised that this was some sort of hymn-book, and in their quaint way they started to sing the Psalms of David. One tragic day Young died. When Smith came to the New Testament, a lovely thing happened. He said, 'I had been working like a mole in the dark for years, and suddenly it was as if the doors flew wide open, and I saw the light, and I met God in Jesus Christ. And the burden of my sin rolled away, and I found new life in Christ.'

Eighteen years after the mutiny of the *Bounty*, a ship from Boston came across the island, and the captain landed. He found a community of men and young people who were quiet and godly, with a grace and peace about them that he had never seen before. Their leader stepped forward, 'My name is Alexander Smith. I am the only remaining member of the ship's company of the *Bounty*. If you want to give me up, you may.' 'I know nothing about that,' said the captain, 'all I know is that these people here need you.' When he got back to the United States he reported that in all his travels he had never seen or met with a people who were so good, so gracious, so loving. How did that happen? There is only one book in the world that would produce a miracle like that.

In the eighteenth century England was in a desperate state. Ignorance and vice stalked through the land. Led by John Wesley, George Whitfield and others, men went through this country of ours on horseback, and everywhere they went they held in their hands one Book. 'God make me a man of one Book,' said John Wesley, and they took the Bible, and read it and explained its message to the common people. A miracle took place.

Even critical historians say that what saved Britain from the bloody revolution that swept through France in the eighteenth century was the revival of pure religion —the influence of the Bible.

It was not until a century later that the whole force, the whole benefit, of that spiritual awakening was felt. During the reign of Queen Victoria a prince from over-seas came to England, and had an audience with Her Majesty. 'Your Majesty,' he said, 'I have seen, and am impressed with the power and glory of this country. I have one question, What in the opinion of Your Majesty is the secret of England's greatness?' The old Queen turned to a table at her side, and picked up very reverently a book, and held it out to the questioner, 'The secret of England's greatness is undoubtedly this Book.'

When we forsake God's Book, we forsake God's laws. And when we forsake God's laws, we forsake God's Son, Jesus Christ. What we need above everything else is a return to the Bible. If we return to the Bible, we shall soon return to the Christ, of whom the Bible speaks. There is no magic, there is no power in this Book of itself. This Book consists of pulp, printer's ink, a bit of leather—maybe cow or goat—a bit of glue from horses' hoofs. The power of this Book is to be found in the theme of the Book. What is the theme? The theme is redemption, new life, forgiveness of sins, for men and women like you and me. Redemption in and through Jesus Christ. Jesus Christ Himself is the theme of this Book.

A theologian, speaking at one of the Hildenborough

Conferences said, 'The Bible is not a book for theologians to argue about; it's not a book for the preacher to get his sermon from.' Then he paused for a moment, and holding the Book in his hand, he said, 'This is a letter from God addressed to you and to me, to introduce us to His Son, Jesus Christ our Lord.'

The reason why some don't believe in the Bible is that they don't believe in Jesus Christ. The reason why they do not believe in the Bible and love the Bible and know the Bible is that they do not believe in Jesus Christ, and love Him and know Him. These two things, the living Word, Jesus Christ, and the written Word of God, the Bible, are married closely together. You can't find one, know one and love one without finding, knowing and loving the other. Of course, you'll find Jesus in the four Gospels: the story of His birth and His death on the cross, His resurrection is told. But you'll find Him too in the Old Testament, in the writings of Moses, the Psalms, the Prophets, then in the Epistles and the Book of Revelation. Wherever you read this Book you will come face to face with our Lord, Jesus Christ, God manifest in the flesh.

CHAPTER THREE

THE HEBREW PROPHETS

Jesus believed in the Hebrew prophets. When a man is a committed disciple of Jesus Christ, he is a man under the discipline of Jesus Christ. He is a scholar in His school. He is following Him as his Lord and Master. The most important thing, is not 'What does this man say?' nor 'What does that man think and believe?' but 'What did Jesus say? What did the Master Himself believe and teach concerning this issue?' Jesus was a teacher sent from God, who spoke the very words of God, and Jesus of Nazareth believed in the Hebrew prophets.

One of the first great utterances that Jesus made, or, if you like, the first great sermon that he preached, was what we call the Sermon on the Mount. At the beginning of that sermon, as if it were one of the most vital utterances He ever made, He said: 'Think not that I am come to destroy the Law, or the Prophets. I am not come to destroy; I am come to fulfil.' To fulfil what? 'To fulfil what Moses wrote in the Law concerning me; to fulfil what the Jewish prophets wrote in their prophesies concerning me.' Then He hastened to add, 'Verily, verily, (truly and earnestly) I say unto you, till heaven and earth pass, one jot or one tittle (one crossing of a "t", one dotting of an "i") shall in no wise pass from the Law, till all be fulfilled.'

For many years now I have been meditating in the four Gospels. I am more impressed than ever before that from his earliest years until His ascension our Lord was constantly conscious that He was deliberately and definitely living a life which was planned, living a life which was prophesied, living a life which was foretold in the writings of Moses, in the writings of the psalmist, David, and in the writings of the Jewish preachers, the Jewish prophets, the major prophets and the minor prophets. All the way through the life and teaching of Jesus this keeps coming out constantly.

Do you remember in the garden of Gethsemane, when they came to arrest Him, Simon Peter drew his sword and smote the high priest's servant and cut off his right ear? Jesus said, 'Put up again thy sword into his place; for all they that take the sword shall perish with the sword. Do you imagine that I cannot now, at this present moment, speak to my Father, and He shall give me presently (immediately, here and now) more than twelve legions of angels, who will wipe not only these evil men from the face of the earth, but all the armies of Rome.' Then He added this: 'But how then shall the Scriptures be fulfilled, that thus it must be? I must suffer; the prophets have foretold it; it is the will of God; therefore I cannot call upon the legions and the hosts of heaven to help me. The Scriptures must be fulfilled.' After His death, after His rising from the dead, having

quoted again and again throughout His public preaching and teaching the words of the prophets, Moses,
David, the major prophets and minor prophets, He met
two disciples, probably Cleopas and his wife, walking
together from Jerusalem to their village home at
Emmaus. As they walked the sun was setting, the
shadows were being thrown ahead on the road, and a
stranger drew near. It was Jesus of Nazareth. Luke says,
'There eyes were holden (closed) that they should not
know Him.' Politely, as He joined them, He asked,
'What manner of communications are these that ye have
one with another as ye walk and are sad?' 'Are you the
only stranger in Jerusalem?' they said. 'Have you not
heard all these things that have come to pass there concerning Jesus of Nazareth, how he was crucified, and how
certain women of our company were early at the sepulchre this morning and said that they had seen a vision
of angels, that said that He was alive? And some of the
men of our company went to the sepulchre, and Him
they saw not, but they found the tomb empty. Beside all
this, we trusted that it had been He, this Jesus of Nazareth, who was going to be the Christ, the Messiah, the
Redeemer of Israel, who would come in and drive out the
armies of Rome and deliver us.'

Very quietly, they still did not know who he was,
Jesus spoke. 'Oh, foolish ones, and slow of heart and
mind to believe all that the prophets have spoken. Ought
not Christ to have suffered these things, and to enter
into His glory? Don't the Hebrew prophets speak not
only of a reigning victorious Christ, but of a suffering
dying Saviour?' Beginning at Moses and all the prophets,

says Luke, He expounded unto them in all the Scriptures the things concerning Himself. Later when they were back in Jerusalem hearing the good news from the disciples, 'The Lord is risen indeed!' Jesus Himself stood in the midst, and said, 'Peace be unto thee.' They were terrified. He said, 'Well, what about giving me something to eat.' He ate in front of them, and they still looked at Him perplexed and worried, so He said, 'You needn't be frightened. You needn't be scared. Look, catch hold of me. Handle me and see—I'm no spirit. A spirit hath not flesh and bones, as ye see I have.' And then He said this: 'This rising again from the dead—these are the very words which I spoke unto you when I was yet with you, pointing out that all these things must be fulfilled which were written in the Law of Moses, and in the Prophets and in the Psalms, concerning me.' Luke writes, 'He opened their understanding, that they might understand the Scriptures.' He said, 'Thus it is written, all about my birth, all about my life, all about my death, all about my resurrection. Thus it is written, and thus it behoved me, the Christ, the Messiah, the Shiloh, to suffer and to enter into glory, to rise again from the dead the third day, so that repentance and remission of sins might be proclaimed throughout all nations, beginning right here in Jerusalem. And you —you here in the upper room this night—you are witnesses of these things. You have actually seen the fulfilment of these ancient prophesies made by the Hebrew prophets, prophets of old. You are going out to witness for me.'

The apostles, in their writing, preaching and teaching,

contantly referred to the Hebrew prophets. Indeed, the Hebrew prophets were their final court of appeal. Matthew, a Jew, who wrote to Jewish readers, in his gospel quotes the Old Testament prophets no less than fifty-three times. When the apostles and our Lord Himself quoted the Old Testament prophets, they always spoke of the prophets as being the mouthpiece of God. For instance, when Matthew tells the story of the conception and birth of our Lord, the angel speaks and says, 'Joseph, thou son of David, fear not to take unto thee Mary, thy wife. This girl that you are engaged to—take and marry her. There's no cause why you should not. She has not been unfaithful to you, for that which is conceived in her is of the Holy Ghost. She shall bring forth a son, and thou shalt call His name Jesus, Jehovah, Saviour. He shall save His people from their sin.' Then this, 'All this is come to pass that it might be fulfilled which was spoken of the Lord by the prophet.' God was the speaker, the prophet was the mouthpiece of God. 'That it might be fulfilled which was spoken of the Lord by the prophet, saying a virgin shall be with child, and shall bring forth a son, and they shall call His name Emmanuel, which being interpreted is, God with us.' Matthew quotes the words of the prophet Isaiah as being the words of God coming through the lips, or the pen, of the prophet Isaiah.

The word 'prophet' in the Bible is used in two senses. First in the sense that we use the word—teacher. A prophet in the Bible is often one who tells forth the word of God, who is the messenger of God. He begins his message in language like this, 'Thus saith the Lord'. In that sense he forthtells or tells out the word of God. There is a second sense in which the word 'prophet' is used. A prophet in the Bible can be someone who fore-tells coming events. Again and again the Hebrew prophets were carried away out of their circumstances, away out from the day and the age in which they lived, by the Spirit and they saw what would take place in future centuries. When the vision was over they came back again to their day and their generation. They either spoke out or they wrote what they had seen and heard in their visions.

Sometimes their prophecies were concerning the Gentile nations—the non-Hebrew nations round about. For instance, when that great city of Babylon was at the height of its power, known as the glory of kingdoms, the mighty city, Isaiah made this statement. 'Oh, Babylon, glory of kingdoms, it shall come to pass unto thee as it was when the Lord judged Sodom and Gomorrah. Behold, no man will dwell in thee from generation to generation. The shepherds will neither graze their flocks there, nor will the wandering Arabs dwell there. Your houses will be desolate from generation to generation. The creatures and wild beasts of the desert shall dwell there. Your houses shall be inhabited by doleful creatures, by the bats and the owls.' How the people must have laughed at him, but less than two centuries afterwards that very thing took place. From that day of the overthrow of Babylon to this day we have with us century after century, the rabble and the ruins of Babylon. Sometimes the prophets prophesied concerning their own kingdom, their own nation, the Hebrews. Moses, a mighty prophet, prophesied that if God's people would turn from the Lord and forsake His Word, and forsake His holy commandments, then, he said 'the Lord will scatter thee among all nations, and He will draw out a sword after thee, and thou shalt know fear and sorrow'.

Throughout history, since God's ancient people forsook the Lord, they have been scattered among the nations of the world. Unlike every other tribe that has been scattered, they have maintained their identity. A sword has been drawn out after them in every year and every generation. The Hebrew prophets also prophesied, not once nor twice but in various ways and in various words, that as sure as they were scattered, God would one day bring them back again, and the nation in Israel would be re-established. In our day the kingdom of Israel has been set up again. I have seen the prophecies made by the ancient Hebrew prophets being fulfilled: cities being built, vines being planted and the desert, through modern irrigation, blossoming like a rose, and prosperity being poured upon God's people, and His people being gathered from the east and from the west.

Undoubtedly, the most fascinating realm of prophecy is concerning their coming Shiloh, their coming Messiah, or the Greek word as we know it—the Christ, meaning God's own anointed one. From the early days in the Old Testament, all the way through Old Testament History, God's prophets have been foretelling the coming of the Messiah. As soon as man had sinned, in Genesis, the message came that a Redeemer would come one day to break the power and tyranny of sin, '. . . and thou shalt bruise his heel, but He—the Messiah—shall

bruise your head, the devil's head. He will by and by
destroy you utterly.' The Old Testament prophets foretold that He would come, and that He would be born
among the descendants of Abraham, a Hebrew, a Jew,
for God swore to His servant Abraham, 'In thee and in
thy seed shall all the nations of the world be blessed.'
Jesus of Nazareth was a Jew, and was recognised immediately as such by everyone who met Him. The
Samaritan woman, as soon as He spoke, looked up and
said, 'How is it that thou, being a Jew, askest drink of
me, which am a woman of Samaria?' The Hebrew
prophets foretold that Jesus would not only be born a
Jew, but would be born of a particular tribe of the Jewish
nation. 'The sceptre shall not pass out of thy house,
Judah.' And so the ancient Jewish people have always
been looking for the coming Messiah, a Jew, born of the
tribe of Judah. That is why Jesus Christ is called 'The
lion of the tribe of Judah'.

The Hebrew prophets named the very family of the
tribe of Judah, in which the Messiah would be born.
The Jews in the time of Jesus knew very well, as they
know today, that the Messiah would be born a descen-
dant of David. When Jesus challenged the teachers and
rulers of the Jews, 'What think ye of Christ? Whose Son
is He?' back came the answer, 'The Son of David.' They
knew it. It had been prophesied by their prophets. Before Christ was born there went out a decree from
Caesar Augustus that all the world should be taxed, and
every man went to his own city to be taxed. And
Joseph went up from Galilee, out of Nazareth, into
Judaea, into the city of David, which is called Bethle-

hem. Why? Because he was of the house and lineage of David. When the angel addressed Joseph in the dream, he said, 'Joseph, thou son of David.'

The Hebrew prophets not only named the family, they even went so far as to name the member of the family through which the Messiah was to be born. Isaiah was the mouthpiece of God in this. Here are his words in the seventh chapter of his prophecy. 'Behold, a virgin shall be with child. She shall bring forth a son, and they shall call the name of that son Emmanuel—God with us.' And that is why we rightly refer to Mary, the mother of Jesus, as the 'blessed virgin Mary'.

Micah went further. He gave the address of where the Messiah was to be born. 'When Jesus was born in Bethlehem of Judaea, in the days of Herod the king, there came wise men from the east to Jerusalem, saying, "Wher is He that is born King of the Jews? For we have seen His star in the east, and we are come to pay Him homage." ' Of course they went to Jerusalem. It was the capital, and you would expect a king to be born in the capital. They went to the palace of King Herod. The crafty old king was disturbed, and all his servants. 'They were troubled,' says Matthew, 'troubled with him.' 'Is there to be some rival to take my place on the throne?' said Herod. He was a professed Jew. 'Can this be the Shiloh, can this be the Christ, the Messiah? Where will I find him? I know, I'll call the chief priests, I'll call the scribes who copy out the sacred writings of the Hebrew prophets, and the Hebrew scriptures. I'll call for them, they'll answer my question.' 'And,' says Matthew, 'when he had gathered all the chief priests and scribes of the people together, he demanded of them where Christ should be born.' Back came the answer like that. 'In Bethlehem of Judaea.' 'Why do you say that?' said Herod. 'Give me chapter and verse for it.' 'Micah, the second chapter. Thus it is written by the prophet Micah, "And thou Bethlehem, in the land of Juda . . ."' If you look at your map, you'll see there are two Bethlehems—one away in the north where Jesus lived, seventy miles away from this one—the other in the south, in the land of Judaea, a stone's throw from Jerusalem. 'And thou Bethlehem . . .', a little tiny hamlet, '. . . and thou Bethlehem, in the land of Juda, art not least among the princes of Juda.' All the great cities are great princes, but you, a little hamlet, are not least among them by any means, 'for out of thee shall come a Governor, that shall rule my people Israel.' 'Herod, you know where the Christ is going to be born—in Bethlehem.' Calling in the wise men, he said, 'I think I can help you. You made a mistake coming here, for this Christ, this wonderful King that you come to do homage to, I'll tell you exactly where He is born. You'll find Him just a few miles away. Go right on till you come to a little hamlet called Bethlehem. You'll find Him there. Now, do me a favour, will you? When you find Him, will you please come and tell me exactly where I'll find Him. I want to come and do Him homage too.' And being warned of God in a dream when they found Him, they departed to their own country, those wise men, another way. And when he saw that he had been tricked, and deceived, he sent forth his men, and they destroyed all the babies in Bethlehem. Hundreds of years before the Jewish prophet

Micah had stated where the Messiah was to be born. And that is exactly where He was born. And the odd thing is this: his father and mother didn't live there. They lived seventy miles away up in the north, up in Galilee, in a despised place, Galilee of the Gentiles, in a place called Nazareth never referred to in the Old Testament. But God put it into the heart of Caesar Augustus to send out a decree that all the world must be taxed. And so there was a big census, for everyone had to go to their own city. That is how it was that Joseph, the husband of Mary, the mother of Jesus, happened on that particular night when Jesus was born to be in that small village, royal David's city, because He was royal David's son, born there, as the prophets centuries before had said He should be born, of a virgin mother in Bethlehem, of the tribe of Judah, a Hebrew of the Hebrews, God's Son, Christ Jesus.

All the details were prophesied years before He was born. The ministry of John the Baptist, 'Behold, I send my messenger before thy face, which shall prepare thy way before thee.' The ministry of Jesus Christ, opening the eyes of the blind and cleansing the leper, raising the dead were all prophesied by the Hebrew prophets. The fact that He should be betrayed by one of His own friends was prophesied in the Old Testament. The fact that He would be sold for a miserable thirty pieces of silver was prophesied in the Old Testament. The fact that the money would be used to purchase the potter's field, where strangers might be buried, were all prophesied in the Old Testament. And King David, who lived seven hundred years before Christ, before Roman crucifixion was even thought of, describes in the twenty-second psalm the death of the Messiah. 'My God, my God, why hast Thou forsaken me?' 'They pierce my hands and my feet, they tell all my bones, they sit and stare upon me, they gamble for my clothes, they cast lots for my vesture. They shake their heads and say, "He trusted in God; let Him now deliver Him, if He will have Him."' The fact that He should rise again from the dead was told by the Old Testament prophets. 'Thou wilt not leave my soul in hell, neither wilt thou suffer thine Holy One to see corruption.' Jesus not only died as the prophets said, but He rose again from the dead as the prophets said. He ascended up to heaven and is at God's right hand. 'Behold, my servant, He shall be extolled and very high. Therefore will I divide Him a portion with the great, and He shall divide the spoil with the strong.' God has raised Jesus from the dead, and set Him at His own right hand in heavenly places, far above all principalities and might and power and dominion, and given Him a name which is above every name, that at the name of Jesus every knee should bow.

In Isaiah 53 we read one of the richest prophecies concerning the death of Christ. How wonderful it is that He should be despised and rejected, that He should be silent at His trial, that He should be found without spot and without blemish, that He should die on the Cross, not for His own sin—He had no sin—but for our sins. His grave was made with the wicked—for undoubtedly a grave was dug with the two common thieves—He was to be buried with the rich in His death. Rich Joseph of Arimathea came and begged the body of Jesus.

A friend of mine is connected with a large firm of biscuit manufacturers. Among the subsidiary companies that my friend directs is one that has been set up by the firm to manufacture the sacred Jewish Passover biscuits. They look exactly like big round water biscuits, but there is no leaven in them. Unleavened bread, the Bible calls them. And the Jews, for whom they make these biscuits, insist on a special factory, away from the main one. When the men go in in the morning they are watched carefully in case anyone might take in a sandwich. Ordinary baker's bread contains leaven, and if leaven got into that factory, the whole factory would be condemned by the Rabbis as unclean, and all the biscuits in the baking would have to be scrapped, and it would have to be cleansed ceremoniously. They have to exercise the utmost care. Very often, unannounced and unheralded, a Rabbi will call, sometimes in the morning and sometimes late in the evening. And he will insist on going right through the factory. A while ago my friend was in his office, and someone came in and said, 'Excuse me, sir. A Rabbi from the United States is here, over in Europe, visiting the Jewish members of the Forces, and he wishes to inspect the factory.' My friend showed the Rabbi around the factory where they bake unleavened bread. When they had finished their inspection they came back to my friend's office, and the Rabbi sat down. On the corner of the desk he saw a book. 'What is that book you have?' 'Oh, that is my Bible,' said my friend. 'You know, Rabbi, we owe the Jews a tremendous lot. We love this book too. And we not only owe you a lot for giving us this book, but we owe you a far greater debt because you've given us the Messiah, the Christ. I am convinced that Jesus of Nazareth is your Messiah, my Saviour, the Saviour of the world.' The Rabbi remained friendly, and they talked together of the books of Moses, the Psalms and the Prophets. Suddenly my friend plucked up his courage, and, looking into the face of the visitor said, 'Rabbi, would you mind if I were to ask you a very personal question?' 'What do you want?' 'Do you mind telling me what you make of the fifty-third chapter of the book of the prophet Isaiah?' 'We never read it in our synagogues. No, we never read it. We do not even have it—it is omitted. We keep it in the Ark, but it's never read.' 'Tell me, Rabbi, why don't the Jewish people read Isaiah fifty-three?' The Rabbi, dropping his voice to a whisper, said, 'We never read the fifty-third chapter of Isaiah, for the man described in that chapter is far too much like your Jesus.'

To meet Jesus you don't have to go to Matthew, Mark, Luke or John, you'll find Him too in the Old Testament. And you'll find Him not only a reigning, victorious, powerful Messiah but able to break the power of sin, to set men and women like you and me free from the love and the practice of sin. You will find Him in Isaiah, the Psalms, and Moses, as a suffering, dying Messiah. 'When we see Him, there is no beauty that we should desire Him . . . despised and rejected of men, a man of sorrows and acquainted with grief; and we hid as it were our faces from Him . . . Surely He hath borne our griefs and carried our sorrows . . . He was wounded for our transgressions, He was bruised for our iniquities, the price of all our peace was heaped upon Him, and with His stripes we are healed. All we like sheep have gone astray; we have turned every one to our own way and the Lord hath laid on Him the iniquity of us all. He shall bear the sins of many; He shall make intercession for the transgressors.' The same Lord Jesus, who died on the Cross, as the Jewish prophets foretold that He would, is encountering you just as He encountered those frightened men in the upper room on the eve of the resurrection. 'Peace be unto you . . . Handle me and see, a spirit hath not flesh and bones, as ye see me have.'

CHAPTER FOUR

THE INNOCENCE OF CHRIST

There are one of two things in connection with a Jewish trial, which may shed some light upon the trial of Jesus Christ.

The accused man had to be accused by two independent witnesses who had not met together for discussion beforehand, they had to give their witness independently of one another. If the witness of these two or more men contradicted, the chief priest (the Lord Chief Justice) declared that there was no case against the prisoner, and he was automatically discharged. If, on the other hand, the two witnesses agreed, then the court would decide whether or not a genuine case of prosecution against the accused could be brought. If this was agreed, then the prisoner was permitted to defend himself, or call witnesses to his defence. In no circumstances in a Jewish court was anyone, including the high priest, permitted to put questions to the prisoner, the answers to which might incriminate him. What is more, the Jewish law never condemned a man simply because he admitted his guilt.

These points help us to understand why Jesus

'answered him never a word'. Jesus kept silent because there had been no proper case laid before the court.

The high priest, in questioning Jesus about his disciples and his doctrine, was in fact breaking the rules of Jewish court, and received, therefore, a just rebuke from the prisoner. (See our Lord's reply in John, chapter 18.)

It was a rule of the Sanhedrin that no trial should be conducted during the night. However, on this occasion this law was broken.

It was also a rule that if a case were heard on one day and the prisoner found guilty, the court would have to adjourn until the following day for verdict to be passed. This accounts for the opening words of Matthew, chapter 27.

The accusation

Jesus of Nazareth did not claim to be *a* son of God, nor did He merely claim to be *the* Son of God, but He claimed that He was *God the Son*. In other words, He claimed no vague divinity, but deity. He said that He was God.

Some said, 'He is a mad man.' No man in his rightful mind would say that he is God. 'He hath a devil and is mad; why hear ye Him?' Others said, 'He is a bad man.' 'Nay, but He deceiveth the people.' 'Thou, being a man, makest thyself God.' A small company of His disciples who, incidentally, knew Him best, said, 'Rabbi, we believe and are sure that thou art the Christ, the Son of the living God.'

It was because Jesus said that He was God that He was brought to trial before the Jewish court, the Sanhedrin, which consisted of seventy members, plus the chairman, the Lord Chief Justice, the high priest, who at that time was named Caiaphas. The whole issue at stake is summed up in the words of the high priest, reported in Matthew, chapter 27, 'I adjure thee by the living God that thou tellest plainly whether thou be the Christ, the Son of the Blessed?'

There were two distinct trials of Jesus: the first before the Jewish court, when the accusation was blasphemy, and the second before the Roman court, under the chairmanship of Pontius Pilate, when the accusation was high treason.

When Christ challenged His disciples, who knew Him more intimately than anyone, with 'Whom say *ye* that I am?' their spokesman, blunt, plain, loving Simon Peter, came back with the answer. There was no 'We venture or suggest, perhaps, without being dogmatic at all, it just may be, Rabbi, that after all, there is something . . .' No, never! That is not apostolic language; that's the weak, anaemic language of our day and generation. 'Rabbi,' said Peter, 'we believe and are sure that thou art the Christ, the Son of the living God.' Did Jesus rebuke him? No, on the contrary, He said quietly, 'Blessed art thou, Simon, son of Jona; flesh and blood hath not revealed this unto thee, but my Father which is in heaven. And upon this truth I am going to build my Church, Simon.'

There was another view. This other group included the elders of the people, and they said, 'He, being a mere man, maketh Himself God. We have a law, and by that law, He ought to die. He is not a good man. He deceiveth the people. He is a deliberate liar.' And they made it their responsibility to put Jesus to death.

If you who have read the Gospel of John carefully, you will have noticed that the miracles of Jesus that John speaks of begin quietly and humbly, Jesus turning water into wine quietly at a very humble wedding feast, and work up to a crescendo, culminating in His own resurrection from the dead. And let me say in passing, that if we can believe and accept the resurrection of Jesus, then we should have no difficulty whatsoever in accepting the lesser miracles. John tells us of the resurrection of Jesus in the twentieth chapter of his Gospel, but the previous miracle of Jesus, according to John, details of which he gives in the eleventh chapter, is the raising of Lazarus of Bethany. And remember, Lazarus had been dead four days when Jesus came; his body was stinking because of the corruption of death, and Jesus raised him from the dead with the words, 'Lazarus, come forth.' And he that was dead came forth. And that miracle of raising a man from the dead, preparing the people undoubtedly for His own death and resurrection that was to take place days afterwards, took place under the very shadow of Jerusalem. Many people of the Jews, influential people from Jerusalem, were there to comfort Martha and Mary, who were not humble peasants, but wealthy people. And people from Jerusalem saw Jesus raise Lazarus.

At the end of the eleventh chapter John says, 'Then many of the Jews which came to Mary, and had seen the thing which Jesus did, believed on Him. But some of them went their ways to the Pharisees, and told them what things Jesus had done.' Raised a man from the dead. Then gathered together the chief priests and the Pharisees, says John, and they called an emergency meeting and they said, 'What are we going to do? This man, this Jesus of Nazareth, He doeth many miracles.' Notice they didn't question the fact that He really did perform miracles. Many today among our religious leaders deny the miracles of Jesus, but not those people who were on the spot. They knew there was no trickery. They admitted it, 'This man doeth many miracles.' 'Now,' they said, 'if we let Him thus alone, all men will believe on Him, and then the Romans will come, and they'll take away both our place and our nation. We shall lose our jobs.' Now do not imagine that that meant that the armies of Rome would invade the country. They had already invaded the country some time before. And Rome treated them pretty well. In the south they had Pontius Pilate, in Judaea, and away in the north they had their own puppet king, Herod. He looked after Galilee, and went on reigning there. Herod also had a palace in Jerusalem. Luke tells us Herod was in Jerusalem at the time of the trial and death of our Saviour. But what the Pharisees were worried about was this: 'This Jesus, if He spoke the word, would lead a revolt, and all the people would be up in arms, and the powers of Rome would come in and there would be awful bloodshed, and we'd lose our jobs and our positions. And this arrangement we have with Rome is very convenient with us just now. What are we going to do?'

John tells us, 'And one of them, named Caiaphas, being the high priest that same year, said unto them, "Ye know nothing at all (you're plain dumb) nor do you consider that it is expedient for us (it is to our advantage) that one man should die for the people, and that the whole nation perish not." ' Then John, with one of his delightful little notes of explanation, says, 'And this spake he not of himself; but being the high priest that year, he prophesied that Jesus should die for that nation; and not for that nation only, but that also He should gather together in one of the children of God that were scattered abroad.'

Do you follow the argument of Caiaphas? He got up and said, 'Here's the issue. We are faced with two evils: on the one hand there is this evil—murdering Jesus of Nazareth. Murder is never right, it's a wicked thing to do, but that's one evil that we're faced with. Now the other evil is this—if we let Jesus alone, all men will believe on Him, the Romans will come and take away our positions. The whole nation will perish. Are we going to stand by and let the nation perish, or are we going to make it our business to see that this Jesus of Nazareth perishes? Now, they are both wrong, but we're faced with two evils; which is the lesser of the two? Well, surely, putting to death Jesus of Nazareth.'

From that time the die was cast; they sought opportunity to destroy Jesus. But it was not easy. The people regarded Jesus of Nazareth as a prophet. A day or two before His trial, multitudes of people from all over the country greeted Him, 'Behold, our King cometh! King Jesus, the Messiah! Blessed is He that cometh in the name of the Lord. Hosanna in the highest!' How they shouted, how they yelled. They were waiting for a word from Jesus, and they would have willingly laid down their lives for Him, had He given such a word. They imagined, quite wrongly, that Jesus had come to set up a kingdom here on earth, a physical kingdom. He had not come for that reason at all. His was a spiritual kingdom, in the hearts of individual men and women.

'Now,' they said, 'if we arrest this Jesus, and if we stone Him to death, or put Him to death by some other means, there will be an uproar among the people, and they will stone us, and they will lynch us, and that will be the end of ourselves, and the end of the nation. It is unthinkable.' So by and by, as Matthew tells us, they had another committee meeting. They said, 'We will not take Him during the feast.' Why not? It was the Jerusalem season, and people from near and far crowded the city. Everyone was talking, in every house and every palace and in every tent, every store and every street, everywhere they were all saying, 'Jesus of Nazareth—is He the Christ? Do our rulers know indeed that this is the Christ? When the Christ comes, will He do more miracles than this man hath done? Surely this is the Christ.' Others said, 'Nay, He deceiveth the people.' Others said, 'He is a mad man, He hath a devil and is mad.' Others replied, 'No, these are not the words of a man that hath a devil. And how can a man that hath a devil open the eyes of a man that is born blind?' The authorities feared that at the feast Jesus would seize the opportunity. They were sacred. He would lead a revolt.

Even while they were meeting, on the very eve of the feast when visitors were crowding into the streets, as they sat in solemn council, they had a real stroke of luck. There was a knock on the door, and the servant came back and said, 'It's one of the disciples of Jesus, Judas Iscariot, and he insists upon seeing His Grace, Caiaphas.' They called him in. 'What do you want?' 'Well,' said Judas, 'I'm no fool. I know what's in your mind. Let's get to business. I'm prepared to betray Jesus of Nazareth to you, provided you make it worth my while. What's it worth to you?' And they covenanted with him for thirty pieces of silver. 'Right,' said Judas. 'You be ready. I know His movements, and I'll lead you and the police officers from the temple court to the place where He is. There'll be no one else around.'

When our Lord instituted the Lord's Supper, He no doubt told the disciples that after they'd sung their hymn and said their prayers and sung their psalms, they would go to pray in the garden of Gethsemane. Then Jesus turned to Judas and said, 'Judas, what thou doest, do quickly.' And he got up and went out. John says that it was night. It was night in his soul too. He went to the palace of the high priest and said, 'It's fixed. Jesus and His disciples are going down to the garden of Gethsemane, across the brook Kedron. There'll be no one around. Send the temple guard. I'll lead them. And listen, I'll go straight to this Jesus. It may be dark—I'll give Him a kiss. Seize Him, but let the others go.'

When the Lord Jesus had finished His prayers, Judas came, and a multitude with swords and staves. Jesus stepped forth and said, 'Whom seek ye?' They answered and said, 'Jesus of Nazareth.' He answered 'I am.' When they heard those words, the very name of God, 'they went backward and fell to the ground.' 'If ye seek me,' said Jesus. 'Let these others go their way.' Then all the disciples forsook Him and fled.

Then, says Matthew, they that had laid hold on Jesus led Him away. They called in at the house of Annas, who was the real power behind the Jewish nation, father-in-law to Caiaphas. What happened there we are not told. Annas sent Him bound to Caiaphas, the high priest, whose palace was near by. There the scribes, the elders, the whole council were assembled, late at night, waiting for Jesus. This was their hour.

What was their particular accusation against the prisoner? One thing towering above everything else— blasphemy. Because He, a mere man, they said, made himself out to be God. He said He was the Messiah, He said He was the Son of God. They had to put up some kind of show of law and order. The high priest asked Jesus concerning His disciples and His doctrine. Said the high priest to himself, 'This countryman will know nothing about Jewish law, or Jewish order. I'll go right ahead.' When the high priest asked Him of His doctrine and His disciples, Jesus answered and said, 'I ever spake openly before the world; I ever taught in the synagogue, and in the temple, where the Jews always assemble, and in private have I said nothing. Why askest thou me? This is against the law. Ask them which heard me. Call your witnesses. Behold, they know what I said.' These words must have disturbed the high priest and made him angry. One of the officers standing by in the dock, John says, smote Jesus with the palm of his hand across His cheek, and said, 'Answerest the high priest so?' Jesus turned to him and said, 'If I have spoken well (if what

I have said is according to Jewish law and Jewish order) why do you smite me? And if I have spoken evil (if what I have said is not true) then bear witness to the truth. You be the first witness against me. But don't smite me.' The high priest said, 'We'd better call the witnesses.'

In came the first witness, and told some story. Then the second witness, who was not allowed to hear the first one, was brought in and was cross-examined. He contradicted some of the things that the first witness had said. Others came in, and again they contradicted one another. The high priest was getting nervous and frightened. Having arrested Jesus, they must get Him into the hands of Pilate before morning, or they would be lynched by the crowd. What was he to do? There was only one thing for it; he would break the rules of the court, he would cross-examine the prisoner himself and force Him to commit Himself.

This is the crisis in the trial of Jesus. Matthew says, 'The high priest arose, and looking at the prisoner said, "I adjure thee by the living God (I put thee on oath before God in heaven) that thou tellest us, art thou the Messiah, the King of Israel? Art thou the Son of God?" ' Humanly speaking Jesus knew that if He said, 'Yes,' He would be signing His own death warrant. Humanly speaking, Jesus knew that if He, at that point, said, 'No,' He might have saved Himself the Cross. But without any hesitation, back came the answer, 'Yes, it is as you say. I am the Messiah, I am the Son of God. Nevertheless, hereafter, ye shall see the Son of man coming in the clouds of heaven, seated on the right hand of power.' And the high priest arose and tore his garments, and said, 'Behold, now, we have heard his blasphemy. What further need have we of witnesses?' They arose and cried, 'He is guilty of death.' And they blind-folded Him, and spat in His face, and smote Him on the cheek, saying, 'Prophesy unto us, thou Messiah, thou Son of God. What is the name of this one who is going to smite you? Take that, and that!'

> *Bearing shame, and scoffing rude;*
> *In my place, condemned, He stood;*
> *Sealed my pardon with His blood;*
> *Hallelujah! What a Saviour!*

The Romans had forbidden the Jews to put any man to death. They had said that no one was to be put to death unless he was first tried before the Roman tribunal. Not, of course, that it would have prevented these men from putting Jesus to death if it had been convenient for them to do so. A few weeks later they took Stephen straight from the Sanhedrin, and dragged him out and stoned him for blasphemy. Then why did not they do it to Jesus? Because there would have been an uprising among the people. Their only hope was to get the Romans to do their dirty work. But how were they going to do it? It would have been a waste of time to go to Pilate and say, 'Pilate, this Jesus says He's the Son of God.' A pagan like Pontius Pilate would have folded his arms, opened his mouth wide, and thrown back his head and laughed. He was not interested in their ideas of religion, whether it was blasphemy or not.

But try as they would, they could not bring up any other charge against Him.

Then one of the inner cabinet had hit upon a clever plan. 'See,' he said, 'here I have it. This Jesus of Nazareth, He says not only that He's God, but He also says He is the Christ, the King of Israel. The *King*. Don't you see? And as loyal subjects of Caesar, we have no king but Caesar. Dear Caesar, how we love him . . . *don't* we? If we take this Jesus before Pilate, and pretend to be loyal to him and loyal to Caesar, and say—it's the truth, isn't it?—He says He's the King, Pilate will have to put Him to death.'

So at the second trial of Jesus of Nazareth, before the Roman court, the question of blasphemy is not mentioned, though at one point they did tell Pilate that Jesus said He was the Son of God, and when Pilate heard that 'he was the more afraid'. Pilate knew that Jesus was innocent, he knew that Jesus of Nazareth was more than a mere man; he knew that the basic reason why the elders had delivered Jesus into his hands was because of envy, jealousy—he could see that it was envy and jealousy that had caused them to do this thing.

They themselves would not go into the judgment hall. If they had done so they would have been defiled, and unable to partake of the Passover. So they stayed outside and hatched their plot for murder, and went ahead with their Passover. Let us be careful of condemning these hypocrites. Our hearts are also full of hypocrisy. Jesus was taken in bound to Pilate. Pilate went out to the elders, it was still early in the morning, and said to them, 'Tell me, what accusation bring ye

THE INNOCENCE OF CHRIST

against this man?' 'Well,' they said, 'if He wasn't a male-factor, a crook, we wouldn't have handed Him over to you, would we?' 'Well,' said Pilate, 'this is the Feast day. I'm busy. I want to have a holiday myself. You take Him, and judge Him according to your law.' They said, 'It's not lawful for us to put any man to death.' 'All right,' he said, 'then come, tell me quickly, what is your accusation against Him?' 'Pilate, it's like this; this man stirreth up the people throughout all Jewry. This man, Jesus, He forbids people to give tribute to Caesar, and says He is a king. We have no king but Caesar.'

Pilate turned and went into the virtually empty judgment hall. Pilate called Jesus to him. Pontius Pilate—a brilliant man—faced Jesus, the Son of God, bound with ropes. Very quietly Pilate put a question, 'Art thou the King of the Jews?' 'It is as you say, and to this end was I born, for this purpose came I forth; but my kingdom is not of this world, else would my servants fight that I should not be delivered into the hands of the Jews; but my kingdom is not from hence.' Pilate knew that the whole thing was a trumped-up charge. He went out and said, 'I find no fault in this man. I'm going to release Him.' But, says the Evangelist, they became more fierce, and they said, 'Listen, He stirreth up the people throughout all Jewry, beginning from Galilee, even to this place.' 'Galilee?' said Pilate. 'Is this man perchance a Galilean?' 'Yes, he's Jesus of Nazareth, of Galilee.' 'Then why have you brought Him to me?' said Pilate. 'He comes from Herod's jurisdiction, your own king. He's in Jerusalem at this time. Take Him away to Herod and let him deal with Him.'

They led Him away, says Luke, to Herod. When Herod saw Jesus, he was exceeding glad. He had hoped for a long time to see Him. He had heard many things of Him, and hoped to see a miracle done by Him. He asked Him many questions, but Jesus answered not a word. Herod and his men clothed Him in a gorgeous robe, and sent Him back again to Pilate.

Again Pilate was faced with the big question, 'What shall I do then with Jesus, which is called Christ?' Again Pilate went out to the people and said, 'I've examined this man in your presence, I've sent Him to Herod, and lo, He has done nothing worthy of death. I'll chastise Him and let Him go.' But they became exceeding fierce, and cried out, 'Crucify Him! Crucify Him!' Again Pilate went in and interviewed Jesus, but just then a messenger rushed in from his wife, Claudia. 'Have thou nothing to do with that just man. I suffered many things this day in a dream because of Him.' Said Pilate, 'I would that I could have nothing to do with Him. I know He's a just man without my wife having dreams and telling me so. But wait a moment . . . of course,' said Pilate to himself, 'the Feast of the Passover . . . the ancient custom that the Governor will release to the people a prisoner whom they would. Here's their popular hero, Jesus of Nazareth. They'll choose Him. I'll let them take their choice between Him and Barabbas, Barabbas lying down there in the dungeon.' Barabbas was a robber, condemned to be crucified.

Pilate went out to the people and said, 'Whom will ye that I release unto you? Barabbas or Jesus, the Messiah, your Christ, your King?' He returned to the judgment hall to wait, but, says the Evangelist, the chief priests persuaded the multitudes that they should ask for Barabbas, and destroy Jesus.

Pilate raising his hand for silence, asked for their verdict. 'Which will ye that I release unto you—Barabbas or Jesus, which is called the Christ?' And they all said unto him, 'Barabbas.' 'Barabbas?' said Pilate. 'What shall I do then with Jesus, which is called your King, the Messiah?' 'Crucify Him! Crucify Him!' 'Why?' said Pilate, 'What evil hath He done? I'll chastise Him and let Him go.' And then it happened. At the back of the crowd a man cupped his hands to his mouth and called, 'Pilate, if you let this man go, you are not Caesar's friend. We have no king but Caesar. Whomsoever calleth himself a king speaketh against Caesar.' Pilate had had one row with Caesar before. The next would be his last.

Pilate called for water, and, says Matthew, he washed his hands before the multitudes, saying, 'I am innocent of the blood of this just person.' All the people answered and said, 'His blood be on us, and on our children.' Then released he Barabbas unto them. While the guilty went out free, the innocent was delivered by Pilate to be crucified, who wrote these words with his own hand, and had them nailed in Hebrew and Greek and in Latin. 'Jesus of Nazareth, the King of the Jews.'

The evidence that Jesus of Nazareth is the Son of God and the King is overwhelming. And He is not only the Son of God, not only the King. Because He died on the Cross, He is the Saviour of the world. As Pilate asked the question two thousand years ago and had to answer it, so, you too must ask and answer precisely the same question, 'What then shall I do with Jesus, which is called the Christ? Shall I fight against Him, saying He's no king, He's no God? Or shall I bow in repentance and humility at His Cross?'

CHAPTER FIVE

THE DEATH OF JESUS CHRIST

Can intelligent people believe in the necessity of the death of our Lord, Jesus Christ? We have seen that He was conceived of the Holy Ghost, born of the Virgin Mary, that He was the King of Israel, God manifested in the flesh. Then why did He die? Did His power fail Him? Was it all a mistake? Did His plans go wrong? A thousand times 'no'. Jesus of Nazareth was unique in that every baby that is born into the world is born to live. Jesus was born, first and foremost, that He might die.

When Mary, the mother of our Lord, and her husband, Joseph, brought the babe Jesus into the temple for His circumcision, a wonderful old prophet, a man of God called Simeon, who was well on in years, was guided by God's Spirit to come into the temple at that very moment. There's something important about Simeon. It had been revealed to him by God that he would not die until he had actually seen with his own eyes the Lord Christ, the Messiah, the Son of God. And when he came into the temple, he took up the babe Jesus in his arms, and he blessed God. 'Lord, now lettest thou thy servant depart in peace, according to thy Word; for mine eyes have seen thy salvation!' Fancy holding God's salvation in your arms! And then, turning to Joseph and Mary, he said this, 'This child is set for the fall and rising again of many in Israel; and for a sign which shall be spoken against.' Then speaking to Mary Simeon said, 'Yea, a sword shall pierce through thy own soul also.'

When I read the story of the crucifixion, and read how Mary stood by beholding, I wonder if the words of Simeon, which she had heard when Jesus was a little babe, came back into her mind. For Luke says that she kept all these things and she pondered them in her heart. 'Yea, a sword shall pierce through thy own soul also.' Although we have in the four Gospels a vivid description of the physical sufferings of our Lord and Saviour, which are described in great detail so that we should meditate upon them, we cannot begin to understand all that Mary, the mother of Jesus, must have suffered out of sympathy and anguish for her son, as He hung naked on a Roman cross, torn and bleeding, with spittle hanging from His beard.

But if we could understand the agony that Mary suffered out of sympathy, even then we should not begin to understand what was going on in the heart of God, the Father Almighty in heaven, as He gave His only begotten Son.

Sometimes it is not the person who is suffering physically who is suffering most. Sometimes the loved ones who watch and stand by helpless, unable to help, suffer even more. 'Yea, a sword shall pierce through thy own soul also.'

When Jesus took Peter, James and John up on to the mountain top, and was transfigured before them, there appeared unto them Moses, representing the Law, and Elijah, representing the Prophets, talking with Jesus, the Messiah, the Christ, the Son of the living God. Luke lets us into a secret: he tells us what they discussed together. They spake together, says Luke, of the death of Jesus, which He would soon accomplish in Jerusalem. And the apostle Peter tells us that the death of Jesus Christ on the Cross is the theme that the prophets desired to look into. It's the mystery that the very angels of God desire, and desire in vain, to understand. The apostle John, in the book of Revelation, tells us that it's the theme of heaven's song. 'Worthy is the Lamb that was slain, they cry, to be exalted thus.'

There is no greater theme in the Bible. Moses, the Psalms, the Prophets, the Gospels, the Epistles, the Revelation; there is no greater theme in the Bible or out of the Bible, in heaven or on earth, than the death of our Lord and Saviour, Jesus Christ. All the way through His life, and all the way through His ministry, the shadow of the Cross fell across His life. Knowing what lay before Him, He set His face like a flint, and went up steadfastly to Jerusalem.

In Caesarea Philippi He challenged the apostles. 'Whom say ye that I am?' Simon Peter, their spokesman answered, 'Rabbi, we believe and are sure that thou art the Christ, the Son of the living God.' Jesus commended Simon, 'Blessed art thou, Simon, son of Jona; my Father has revealed this to you.' From that time, Matthew says, Jesus started to tell the disciples how He must go to

Jerusalem, and there be betrayed, there He must suffer, and there He must die. Simon Peter spoke up again, and he took Jesus and began to rebuke Him, 'Be it far from thee, Lord, this shall not happen unto thee. This is defeatist talk, about suffering and dying on a cross; we don't like it, we don't want that sort of talk. We believe in a Messiah who will sit in judgment and power upon a throne and drive out the armies of Rome. Speak no more about the cross and about dying, Lord.' Jesus, who a moment before had said, 'Blessed art thou, Simon, son of Jona,' turned on him and said, 'Get thee behind me, Satan.' To whom was Jesus speaking? Peter. What did He say? 'Get thee behind me, Satan. Thou art an offence, a stumbling-block; thou savourest not the things that be of God, thou savourest the things that be of men.'

Jesus had before Him all the time, as the climax of His coming into the world, His Cross, His passion, His death, His resurrection. Simon Peter in the garden of Gethsemane, drew his sword and started to lash out, and smote Malchus, servant of the high priest, and cut off his ear. Jesus said, 'Put up again thy sword into his sheath. The cup which my Father hath given me to drink, shall I not drink it? How then shall the scripture be fulfilled, that thus it must be? I must die, and for this purpose I came into the world.'

Long before He went to the Cross, Jesus of Nazareth made this emphatic statement, 'The Son of man came to give His life a ransom in the place of many.' Why did He come? To give His life, to die, in the place of many.

On the night He was betrayed, He reminded His disciples of His purpose again. He took the bread and broke it, and said, 'This is my body.' He took the wine, and poured it out, and said, 'This is my blood, shed for the remission of sin.'

Jesus did not die on the Cross, as has been suggested, to set us an example of how we ought to face death. Indeed, if you are looking for an example of how you ought to face death, read the lives of the martyrs. One was flung to the wild beasts in Rome, with the crowds yelling for his blood, as the wild beasts rushed on him. What did he do? 'Let me be food for these wild beasts, if only God be glorified.' Or think again, as the flames start to burn the bodies of the martyrs. Hear one man cry through the flames and smoke, 'Be of good cheer, brothers, be of good cheer.'

When you come to study the four Gospels to see how Jesus faced the Cross, you get a different picture. Sometimes people who have to face major surgery suffer far more in anticipation than they do during and immediately after the operation. Have you ever paused to think of what it meant to be Jesus of Nazareth, a sensitive man, and a real man He was, knowing what He would have to face in the Cross? See Him in the garden of Gethsemane, praying for strength, calling Peter, James and John to stand by Him and pray with Him for a while. When He found them fast asleep He went away and prayed again the more earnestly. He sweated, as it were, great drops of blood. 'If it be possible, my Father, let this cup pass from me; nevertheless, not as I will, but as thou wilt.' Jesus shrank from death, He shrank from the Cross.

You might ask, why did the disciples of Jesus face
death with triumph, while our Lord faced His death
with fear? I think this is the answer: the disciples of
Jesus who are called to face death, face physical, bodily
suffering, but they face spiritual light, glory, life eternal.
But when Jesus faced the Cross, He faced not only
physical agony, physical death, not only mental anguish,
but He faced an evil darkness and spiritual death that
no true child of God will ever know.

Why? Because there on the Cross He, who knew no
sin, innocent, the Lamb without spot, without blemish,
was made sin, made a sin offering for us. He bore our
sins in His own body on the tree.

When Jesus died, He did not die to prove and demon-
strate His love towards us. Indeed, if Jesus died only to
prove His love, then He died in vain, He laid down
His life wastefully. He did not even prove His point.

Can you imagine a fellow and girl walking along one
evening by the riverside? He is trying desperately hard
to persuade her that he really loves her, that he cares,
but somehow she won't be convinced, and he gets het
up about it. Really worried. Suddenly he has an inspiration. He looks into the water, and he bears in mind that
he is not a swimmer, and he realises that the water is
deep, and he says to himself, 'I've got it!' Then he turns
to his girl and says, 'I am going to prove to you that I
love you by throwing myself into the river.' So he takes
a header, and all that comes up are a few bubbles. Poor
chap! Do you really think that he's proved his love? He
certainly has not. What has he proved? He's proved
that he's emotionally unstable, and not worthy to marry

any girl.

I heard a man say that the only reason Jesus died on the Cross was to prove that He loved us. Well, if that's all He died for, He did not prove the point at all, He wasted His life.

But wait, supposing as they walked together, the girl stumbled and fell, and supposing, realising his inability to swim and not caring for his own life, the young fellow flings himself in, and with great difficulty he gets her to the bank, her life saved, but in so doing he loses his own life, he dies so that she might live. Now what's he done? First and foremost, towering above everything else, he has saved her, delivered her from death. He has died and laid down his life that she might live. Yes, but as an important by-product, he has also proved that he loved her, that he cared for her.

Jesus Christ rose again from the dead. I don't want to give you the impression that we're talking about a dead Saviour. We are talking about His death just now, but He is alive now, and He is here. And if you could see Him, as Thomas saw Him, you would see the print of the nails in His hands and feet. And if you could hear Him, I think you would hear Him say to you, 'Greater love hath no man than this, that a man lay down his life for his friends.' 'Behold and see, is there any sorrow like unto my sorrow?' 'Is it nothing to you all ye that pass by?'

At one of the Royal Albert Hall meetings, a student nurse was invited to come one night. She didn't know what it was about. She said afterwards, 'I enjoyed the singing. Then when Tom Rees started to speak, I must

confess I didn't understand most of it. I don't know
now what it was all about.' But then she said, 'All I
know is this, that before he was through talking about
whatever he was talking about, I saw Jesus Christ lifted
up on the Cross, dying in agony for me. And I saw for
the first time that it was *my* sin that nailed Jesus to the
Cross. In the silence at the end of the address, I committed my life to Jesus Christ.'

God in Christ willingly, gladly, out of love for you
and your soul, when He might have gone back to heaven
in glory, went voluntarily to the Cross. No man took His
life from Him; He laid it down of Himself, out of love
for you, and the Father's will.

The Bible is as plain as day. It was *our* sin, it was *our*
iniquity, it was *our* transgressions, that nailed God's Son
to the Cross. 'There was none other good enough to pay
the price of sin; He only could unlock the gate of heaven
and let us in.' Because He faced death and suffered
death, we can know redemption and justification and
new life given through Christ.

The Bible states emphatically, 'Cursed is everyone
that continueth not in all things that are written in the
book of the law, to do them.' Every man, every woman,
out of Christ is under the curse of God. We have broken
God's holy Law. But Paul explains it so beautifully, so
that a little child could understand. He says, 'Yes, although we are cursed by our sins, cursed of God because
of our sin, Christ Jesus has redeemed us, He has released
us, He has brought us back again from the curse of the
Law.' How? By being made 'Curse' for us. For it is
written, 'Cursed is everyone that hangeth upon a tree.'

When Jesus was nailed to the tree at Golgotha, the place of the skull, He was cursed of God, for you and for me, that the blessing of God might rest on you, that you might know forgiveness of sin and the smile of heaven upon your heart. I want to ask have you ever honestly, deep down in your heart, as a mature, thoughtful man or woman, come to the foot of the Cross, and looked into the face of Jesus, dying there for you? Have you ever said, 'He is the Son of God, that loved me and gave Himself for me. God, be merciful to me, a sinner?'

CHAPTER SIX

THE RESURRECTION

Can an intelligent person believe in the resurrection of Jesus Christ? You may say, 'I don't see that it makes any real difference in this space age, whether the resurrection of Jesus is fact or fiction. It happened or did not happen nearly two thousand years ago, and cannot have much practical bearing upon life today.' On the contrary, whether or not Christ rose again from the dead makes all the difference to people like ourselves today. If Jesus did not rise from the dead, then the whole of the Christian religion, and modern civilisation as we know it, which has its roots in the Christian religion, is built and founded upon a lie, a gross deception. On the other hand, if Jesus did rise from the dead, then we must come to the feet of Christ, as Thomas of old did, and worship Him with, 'My Lord and my God.'

The Christian religion stands or falls by the resurrection of Jesus Christ. Our hope of eternal life stands or falls by the resurrection. If Jesus did rise again from the dead, then this life is a passing phase, the preparation and training for the real life, the permanent life, beyond the grave. If Jesus did not rise from the dead, then when we die we shall snuff out like animals. And, as St. Paul says, 'We are of all men most miserable'— we get no kick out of this life, and there's nothing but nothingness beyond the grave. As for our faith, our doctrine, it's vain, said St. Paul, it's empty, if Jesus didn't rise again from the dead.

And so it matters intensely whether the resurrection of Jesus Christ is, as one person suggested, merely fiction on the one hand, or whether it is an established fact of history on the other.

Dr. Arnold, sometime headmaster of Rugby School, and a wise man, who weighed his words carefully, said about the resurrection of Christ: 'The resurrection of Jesus Christ from the dead is one of the best attested facts in the whole of human history.' Dr. Arnold spoke the truth.

If you will read, as I have done, the many arguments that have been produced by men in years past *against* the resurrection, each isolated argument as you read it and think about it, is overwhelmingly convincing. On the other hand, if you will collect, as I have done, the many infallible proofs of the resurrection of Jesus, and take each one of those proofs and isolate it from the others, each isolated single proof *for* the resurrection of Jesus will impress you as being rather unconvincing. But wait! Start adding up and comparing the arguments that have been produced against the resurrection of Jesus, and you will find that the whole lot will contradict one another, and the arguments against the resurrection of Jesus Christ will collapse like a pack of cards. On the other hand, if you will take together the

arguments for the resurrection of Jesus, although isolated and alone they may seem a little unconvincing,
start adding them up and you will find that you pile up
for yourself overwhelming evidence, and you will start
to understand what St. Luke meant when he talked about
'Jesus, our Lord, who showed Himself to the apostles
after His death, after His passion, by many infallible
proofs.'

The arguments for the resurrection of Jesus Christ
are many. I wish I could take a score of them but I will
discuss with you four reasons why I believe an intelligent
person can accept the resurrection of Jesus Christ.

In the first place, I believe an intelligent person can
believe in the resurrection of Jesus Christ because of the
evidence of the four Gospels. These four Gospels bear
the names of Matthew, Mark, Luke and John. Do not
let us worry for the moment whether or not these men
did write these books. We have four records of the birth
and the life and the death and the resurrection of Jesus.
That is an indisputable fact. And this too is indisputable: the climax of each story in the four Gospels is the
resurrection, the rising again from the dead of Jesus of
Nazareth, who in each case is the central character in the
story.

If you will read the four Gospels with an open mind,
trying to forget your pre-conceived notions and ideas,
just reading them like an ordinary book, not trying to
make yourself believe on one hand, not trying to look
for difficulties and problems on the other hand, I think
you will come to this conclusion that here are four more
or less independent accounts of the life and the death

and the resurrection of Jesus of Nazareth. You will come to that conclusion because on your first reading of the four Gospels, you will possibly have stumbled and been not a little puzzled by apparent contradictions between the four records, However, as you read and re-read —and who can understand the Gospels at one reading?— you will become more and more impressed with the deep underlying harmony existing between them. I have noticed this, that the people who are most worried about the apparent contradictions are invariably the people who know least about the Gospels. On the other hand, the people who know most about the four Gospels are always most impressed by the underlying harmony existing between the four records.

As you read, you will say to yourself, as I said to my-self long ago—and I have not always believed in Jesus Christ, and I have not always believed in the Bible— that the sort of evidence, witness and story that these four men give is the sort of evidence and witness that four people would give of any event that they had seen or heard of. People who are experts in examining witnesses are able quickly to detect in their cross-examination in the comparison between this witness and that witness what is false, what is imagined, what is rumour, compared with that which is true, solid and acceptable fact. But you say, 'I am not an expert, I am not accustomed to examining witnesses, therefore I cannot judge.' On the contrary, you are the better able to judge. I need not remind you, that when the law courts want to decide some very very important issue, they do not call the experts, they call a bunch of Tom, Dick and

Harrys, Marys and Janes like you and me, and they constitute us into a jury. They say, and rightly so, that ordinary, unskilled people, have a wonderful gift of being able to discern that which is real from that which is false.

If you are prepared to face this, that as you read and re-read the four Gospels, you will conclude, 'These men are each telling their own story from their own point of view. This is truth.' And the apparent contradictions that they make are the sort of contradictions that four different people would make who are each telling what they saw from their own particular point of view. And though they may appear to contradict in detail, in main point and main issue, they are agreed.

If these four people whom we call Matthew, Mark, Luke and John got together round a committee table and decided what they were going to write, and fabricated the story of the life, death and resurrection of Jesus Christ, and compared notes with one another, you would have had surface harmony, but as you dug deep, serious contradictions. But you don't have that for these four people did not compare notes. They each wrote what they knew to be the truth, either from seeing it, or from talking and reporting from people who saw these events.

One wise man, when he had concluded reading Luke's version of the resurrection of Jesus Christ, said, 'Luke was either a greater poet, a greater creative genius than William Shakespeare, or he didn't fabricate the story at all; he was writing plain truth.' I submit to you that the record of the four Gospels concerning the resurrection of Jesus Christ is overwhelming. It leads me to believe that

Jesus rose from the dead.

Here's the second point: I believe in the resurrection of Jesus Christ because of the amazing transformation that took place in the lives of the apostles after the resurrection. When you go through the four Gospels, and study the lives of the apostles, his special messengers (that's what the word 'apostle' means), you will see what a miserable bunch they were. They were always quarrelling among themselves, 'I'm more important than you are.' And they kept an eye on the purse all the time. When Jesus said, 'I want to buy bread for this great multitude of people; we're going to give them a feast,' the apostles panicked. They looked at Judas holding the kitty and they said, 'Rabbi, 200 pennyworth is not sufficient to feed them, that each of them may take a little.' They were scared that Jesus was going to raid their reserves.

And they were powerless. Jesus went up on to the mountain top to pray, and when He came back, there they were, lifting their hands and making signs, and using the name of Jesus, trying to cast the devil out of a lad. And they could not do it. When Jesus came, He cast the Devil out, and they said, 'Lord, why could we not cast him out?'

And scared! Of course, they were all very brave in the upper room. 'Though all men deny thee, Lord, yet will not I.' And it was not only Peter who said that; they all said, 'Hear, hear. Amen.' And what about Peter? It was only a girl—a saucy-looking girl, with a dimple in one cheek, I don't doubt. When Peter was cold and wanted to get into the high priest's house after Jesus had been arrested, his friend John, who knew the high priest, let him in. The girl looked at Peter and said, 'You're one of His disciples, aren't you' 'Me?' said Peter. 'Don't know what you're talking about.' 'Oh yes,' she said, 'you can't hide your Yorkshire—I mean, your Galilean accent.' He cursed. An apostle, mark you. 'I don't know what you're talking about.'

Now turn the pages over to the beginning of the Acts of the Apostles, and you read about the same men. What a difference! Greedy? No longer. Here's Peter talking: 'Silver and gold have I none'—of course, Judas had made off with it all, but he did not care about that now—but 'such as I have, give I thee'. Here is something tremendous. In the Gospels: 'Lord, why could we not cast him out?' In the Acts: 'In the name of Jesus of Nazareth, rise and walk.' And they went everywhere, says Luke, turning the world upside down. Actually they did not—they helped put it the right way up. Peter, who denied Jesus with oaths and curses when a pretty girl pointed her finger at him, stands up a few weeks later before the entire Jewish Parliament, 'The same Jesus, whom ye crucified, God hath raised up to be a Prince and a Saviour.' The same man? Yes, the same man.

It is hard to believe that the apostles of the gospels and the apostles of the Acts were the same characters. Why were they so different? There is only one answer to that question. Their Master had not only died for them, but He had risen again from the dead, and they had met Him, they had eaten with Him, they had handled Him, they had talked with Him, and they knew He was alive, by many infallible proofs. And wherever they went, throughout Jerusalem, Judaea, Galilee and the whole world, the very heart and core of their gospel was this: 'God hath raised this Jesus, whom ye crucified, from the dead, to be a Prince and a Saviour.' The resurrection was the heart and the core of the apostolic Gospel. This is the message that the world needs to hear again.

When the apostles said that Jesus was alive, they either spoke the truth, or they told a lie. They were either speaking the truth when they said, 'We've seen Him, we are witnesses,' or they were telling lies. But when do people lie? Why do people lie? A small boy was asked what a lie was, and seeking to impress the Scripture master he thought he would quote the Bible in his answer. 'Please, sir, a lie is an abomination unto the Lord, but a very present help in trouble.' A misquotation, but when do people lie? When they want to gain something by lying. Do people lie when they know they are going to lose by telling a lie? No. Do people lie when they know the lie is going to cost them life itself? No. The apostles, humanly speaking, had nothing to gain by saying Jesus was alive if He was not. And more than one of these apostles died rather than recant. They died because they said, 'We know, beyond all doubt, that Jesus Christ is alive. We've seen Him, we've talked with Him, we've touched Him, He's eaten with us; we gave Him fish and a bit of honeycomb. We will not recant, but we will die for what we know to be the truth.'

The apostles were transformed characters because Jesus rose from the dead. They knew that Jesus was alive; they met Him; He changed their lives. Christianity is not based on a lie; it is based upon an established fact.

These people met Him individually; they met Him in twos and threes; they met Him on one occasion when no less than five hundred people were all gathered together and they all saw Him.

Here is the third thing. Intelligent people can believe in the resurrection of Jesus Christ because of the empty tomb. And when I say 'empty tomb', I mean on the third day, the sepulchre of Jesus was empty, as far as His body was concerned. It was not, however, completely empty, for the grave clothes in which His body had been lovingly wrapped by Joseph of Arimathea, and the women who helped him, were left there in the tomb.

It has been my privilege very early one morning to go alone to this lovely garden outside Jerusalem; the sun was rising, and there was no sound except for the song of the birds. I took my Bible with me, and I reconstructed the whole event. Very reverently I stooped down and went where Peter, followed by John, went. I looked at the spot where Jesus had lain, and I saw the place where the grave clothes were left. John says, 'And the napkin that was bound about His head, not lying with the linen clothes, but folded up in an orderly manner and laid aside.' His body? Gone!

It is an indisputable fact that on the third day the tomb of Jesus of Nazareth was empty, but what had happened? Various suggestions have been made.

The first suggestion is that perhaps Jesus did not die; that on the Cross, through the heat of the sun, hanging there, through loss of blood, He fainted and they only thought He was dead. And perhaps the cool tomb and the fragrant spices revived Him, and He came out, and they thought He had risen from the dead, when in fact He had never died. Josephus tells the story of a Roman officer to whom that actually did happen. That is not what happened to Jesus. When the Roman soldiers, who were so quick and experienced to recognise death, came to take the three bodies down from the three crosses, they came to the thieves and broke the legs of the first, and broke the legs of the second. They came to Jesus, but they broke not His legs, because He was dead already. But to make sure that He was dead, says the Evangelist, one of the soldiers took a spear and pierced His side. Many of the early Christians were there watching it. Moreover, when Joseph of Arimathea, who himself was a friend and a disciple of Jesus, went to Pilate and begged for the body of Jesus, Pilate marvelled that He was dead so soon already. You remember he sent for the Roman officer, the centurion who was in charge of the cruci-fixion, and enquired, 'Is it a fact that Jesus of Nazareth is already dead?' It would have cost the Roman officer his life if he had made a mistake. Without any hesitation, he told Pilate, 'Undoubtedly he is dead.'

Do you think those loving hands that placed His body in the precious linen cloth would have left Him in the tomb if there had been any sign of life?

Did the Jews come and steal the body? What would be their motive? If the Jews stole the body of Jesus, when the story of the resurrection spread, why did not they prick the bubble once and for all. 'Alive? Come and see the corpse.' The Jews were intent on making certain that the body was not stolen. Immediately after our Lord had been buried, the scribes and Pharisees came together unto Pilate. 'Sir, we remember that this deceiver said while He was yet alive, "After three days I will rise again from the dead." Pilate, command therefore that the sepulchre be made sure, lest His disciples come in the night and steal Him away, and say to the people that He is risen from the dead, and the last error shall be worse than the first.' 'Go your way,' said Pilate. 'Ye have a watch. Make it as sure as you can.' The Jews did not steal the body; they would have given any sum to find it.

Perhaps His disciples stole it? Did they? Do you really believe Christianity is founded upon a lie? How do you account for the amazing transformation in the lives of these men, if they had lied about it all? Impossible!

'Perhaps thieves stole the body?' The only really valuable thing in the tomb was the linen clothes in which His body had been wrapped, and they were very valuable. They were worth stealing, but whoever removed the body left them behind. The clothes were left, neatly folded.

As far as I can understand, as later His body passed through closed doors, so His body passed through the linen cloth and the napkin bound about His head. The only way of accounting for the empty tomb is by accepting what the Gospel writer says. He rose from the dead.

In the fourth place, I believe that Jesus rose from the dead because the guards were not put to death. After His death and burial, the chief priests and Pharisees had the authority of Pilate to put a guard on the tomb. They took the temple guard, and they put a watch over the tomb, a watch by day and by night. The high priest, undoubtedly using his own seal, sealed the stone, and they made it as sure as they could. If people came to steal the body of Jesus Christ, why did not the guard arrest them? If, as they said, they had fallen asleep on military duty, which was punishable in those days by death, why were not they put to death?

Let me tell you what happened. Very early in the morning came Mary Magdalene and the other women to the sepulchre, and the angel of the Lord descended from heaven, and came and rolled back the stone of the door and he sat upon it. His face was radiant, white as snow, and for fear the keepers did shake, and became as dead men. The angel said unto the women, 'Fear not ye, for I know that ye seek Jesus. He is not here, He is risen. Come and see the place where the Lord lay, and go and tell His disciples that He is risen from the dead. Lo, He goeth before you into Galilee. There ye shall see Him. Lo, I have told you.' The women, full of joy, ran from the sepulchre to tell the disciples.

Can an intelligent person *not* believe in the resurrection of Jesus Christ?

CHAPTER SEVEN

DEITY OF JESUS OF NAZARETH

This is a subject that has puzzled thoughtful people for generations: Can intelligent people believe in the deity of Jesus of Nazareth? When we talk about the deity of Jesus, we mean the Godhead of Jesus. Can we believe that Jesus, the carpenter of Nazareth, was indeed God? That is God in human form. Was Jesus, as the Creed says, conceived of the Holy Ghost, born of the Virgin Mary, or was he the illegitimate son of Mary? Undoubtedly Jesus of Nazareth was the most explosive personality that ever walked across the pages of history. He was either the most wonderful personality, demanding our worship, or He was the greatest impostor and fraud.

I was taught authoritatively that no doctor or man of science believed in the virgin birth. Those who told me were appallingly ignorant, as I was myself, of the four Gospels. And not only were they ignorant of the four Gospels but they were ignorant of the opinions of many distinguished men and women. I have among my friends doctors, and not a few men of science, who firmly believe that our Lord was conceived by the Holy Ghost, born of the Virgin Mary.

I have preached on a number of occasions in a famous Presbyterian church in Baltimore, in the United States. The first time I preached in that church was in 1937. The minister, Dr. Roland Phillips, on the opening night of my services called on one of the elders to open the meeting with prayer. There came forward to the Bible desk an old man with snow-white hair. He was introduced as Dr. Kelly, and as soon as he started to pray I thought this man knows God. Afterwards Dr. Phillips said 'I should have introduced you. That is Dr. Howard Kelly, one of the world's most brilliant surgeons.'

Today I have a book in my library at home, written by Dr. Kelly, with the title *A scientist's belief in the Bible.* The title of chapter 6 is 'Why I believe in the virgin birth.'

What exactly did Jesus of Nazareth, the carpenter, claim for Himself? Then, what were the reactions of the people who heard His claims? Thirdly, what evidence did Jesus Himself produce, which is acceptable to intelligent, open-minded, men and women?

I was once invited to speak at a British University Christian Union. A young woman came to me. She was a third-year student, and she said, 'Mr. Rees, you are acquainted with the fact, aren't you, that the idea of Jesus being anything more than a mere man, this idea of Jesus being God, wasn't invented until the second or perhaps the third century. You know that, don't you?' I looked at her in amazement. I said, 'Madam, you stagger me!' How could any intelligent person ever read the four Gospels and make such a statement? What did Jesus say about Himself? First, that He was the Christ,

God's anointed one, the man for whom the Jews of His day were looking. They were looking for a superman, a God-man, and they knew that when the Messiah arrived, He would be God the Son, manifested in human form. Their prophets told them, 'He shall be called Emmanuel,' which means God with us. 'His name shall be called Wonderful, the Prince of Peace, the everlasting Father.' In the fourth chapter of his Gospel, John tells us how the Lord Jesus Christ spoke to a sinful woman, a Samaritan. In the course of the conversation realising that she could no longer deceive Jesus, she looked up and said, 'Sir, we Samaritans know that the Messiah cometh, who is called the Christ, and when He is come we will know Him, for He will tell us all things.' And the words were scarcely out of her lips when back came the reply from Jesus, 'I that speak unto thee am He.'

In the fifth chapter of John's Gospel, our Lord healed the impotent paralysed man at the side of the pool at Bethsaida on the Sabbath day commanding him, 'Rise, take up thy bed and walk.' And the man, paralysed for forty-eight years, lifted up his couch and walked. The Jews, seeing a man carrying a burden on the holy Sabbath day, crowded round and said, 'It is the Sabbath day. It is not lawful for thee to carry thy bed.' 'No,' said the man, 'but He that made me whole, the same said unto me, "Rise, take up thy bed and walk."' 'What man is that that saith, "Take up thy bed and walk"?' But the man did not know that it was Jesus. Later, however, he discovered, and John says that the man went and told the Jews that it was Jesus who had made him whole. John says, 'Therefore did the Jews persecute Jesus, and sought to slay Him.' Why? 'Because He had done these things on the Sabbath day.' Jesus said, 'My Father worketh hitherto, and I work. My Father causeth the sun to rise and the sun to set, He causeth the flowers to open their petals on the Sabbath day. My Father worketh hitherto.' The Jews hardly heard except the first two words of His answer, 'My Father'. The next verse says, 'Therefore the Jews sought the more to kill Him, because He not only had broken the Sabbath, but said also that God was His Father, making Himself equal with God.'

No less than 187 times in the four Gospels Jesus used this expression, 'My Father'. I know what those words meant to the Jews. I know what those words were intended to mean by Jesus. That God was His own particular Father, that He was God's only begotten Son, in a unique special way. The first recorded words of Jesus bear out this truth. When the child Jesus, Luke tells us in the second chapter of his Gospel, was twelve years of age, He went with Joseph and His Mother to Jerusalem. At the end of the feast they returned and went a day's journey, supposing the child Jesus to be in the company. They sought Him among their kinsfolk and their acquaintances, but found Him not. They went back, says Luke, to Jerusalem, seeking Him and after three days of agony and anguish they found Him in the temple, among the doctors, asking them and answering their questions. Mary his mother said, 'Son, why hast thou dealt thus with us? Thy father (the carpenter of Nazareth) and I have sought thee sorrowing.' 'How is it that ye sought me? Know ye not that I must be about my Father's business?' In the first words recorded from the lips of Jesus of Nazareth, He disclaims the carpenter as His father, and He uses the expression, 'My Father'.

Almost the first thing He did when He commenced His ministry was to go into the temple. John tells us about it in the second chapter of his Gospel. He drove out those who bought and sold, and put His shoulder to the changers of money, and overthrew the tables, and said to the people in anger, with a whip in His hand, 'Make not my Father's house a house of merchandise.' What did He call the temple? My Father's house. No wonder they crowded round. No wonder they said, 'By what authority do you call this temple "*your* Father's house"?' He knew exactly what He was saying, and exactly why He was saying it. Read His words in the fifth chapter of John's Gospel. 'All men,' said Jesus, 'should honour the Son, even as they honour the Father. He that honoureth not the Son, honoureth not the Father which hath sent Him.' Did the carpenter of Nazareth claim equal honour with Jehovah, God? Yes. Again in the same chapter, 'The Father judgeth no man, but hath committed all judgment unto the Son. Marvel not at this, for the day is coming when all that are in the grace shall hear His voice. And they that hear shall rise and come forth; they that have done good unto the resurrection of life, and they that have done evil unto the resurrection of damnation. I, the Son, am the judge of all the world.'

In the eighth chapter of John's Gospel: 'I, the preacher from Nazareth, truly and earnestly say unto you, if a man will keep my sayings, he shall never see death.' And the Jews folded their arms and said, 'Abraham is dead, and the prophets are dead, and thou sayest, "If a man keep my sayings, he shall never see death." Whom makest thou thyself?' 'Truly and earnestly I say unto you, your father Abraham rejoiced to see my day. By the spirit of prophecy, he saw the coming of the Messiah. Your father Abraham rejoiced to see my day, and he was right.' 'Now,' they said, 'we know you're mad and possessed of the devil. Why, you're not yet fifty years old, and hast thou seen Abraham? Jesus, the carpenter of Nazareth?' He answered, 'Truly and earnestly, I say unto you, before Abraham was, I am.' 'Then took they up stones to cast at Him, but Jesus hid Himself, and so passed by.'

Read again, if you will, in the tenth chapter of John's Gospel, how one day when Jesus was walking in Solomon's porch in the temple the Jews came and said, 'How long dost thou make us to doubt? Art thou the Christ, the Messiah?' 'I have told you already, and ye believed not, and ye believe not because ye are not of my sheep, as I said unto you. My sheep hear my voice, and I give to my sheep,' said Jesus, 'eternal life, and they shall never perish, neither shall any man pluck my sheep out of my hand. My Father, who gave them unto me, He is greater than all, and none shall pluck them out of my Father's hand. I and my Father are one.' Then once again they took up stones to cast at Him. But our Lord Jesus Christ looked at them, and here are His words, 'Many good works have I shewed you from my Father; for which of those good works do ye stone me?' They answered, 'For a good work we stone thee not, but for blasphemy, and because thou, being only a man, makest thyself God.'

The one who suggests that the idea of Jesus as God was not invented until after His death, is totally ignorant of the four Gospels.

In the nineteenth chapter of his Gospel, John reminds us that during the trial of Jesus Pilate found no fault with Him. Pilate said, therefore, to the Jews, 'I find no fault in Him.' And the Jews said, 'Crucify Him! Crucify Him!' Pilate said unto them, 'Take ye Him, and crucify Him.' Back came the answer from the Jews. 'We have a law, and by our law He ought to die, because He made Himself the Son of God.' And when Pilate heard these words, he was the more afraid. Matthew, who gives most detail concerning the trial of Jesus, tells us that the crisis in the trial of Jesus before the Jewish Sanhedrin came when the high priest, the chairman of the court, put a leading question to the prisoner. 'I adjure thee by the living God,' said the high priest, 'that thou tell us whether thou be the Christ, the Son of God.' Back came the answer. 'Thou hast said.' And then He added this. 'Hereafter shall ye—you high priest, who are my judge this day—you shall see me, the Son of man, sitting on the right hand of power, and coming in the clouds of heaven. That day you'll be the prisoner, and I'll be the judge on the throne. Things will be reversed then.' And the high priest arose and tore his garments, says Matthew, and speaking to the assembled company, said, 'What think ye? We have heard His blasphemy.' And they arose and said, 'He is worthy of death,' and they condemned Him to die. Why? Because He, being (they said) a mere man, made out himself to be God.

Jesus of Nazareth was either a deliberate deceiver, a

fraud and a humbug, saying that He was God when He knew very well He wasn't, or He was deluded and a mad man, or if He wasn't a bad man and he wasn't a mad man, then He *was* God's Son. The Jewish rulers and the Pharisees took the view that He was a bad man. 'He deceiveth the people. He, being a mere man, maketh Himself out to be God. But we have a law, and by our law He ought to die for this blasphemy.' They said He was a bad man, so they set to work to slay Him, to persecute Him, to put Him to death, and they did not rest until they had done it.

A considerable section of people took a different view. They said, 'He himself is deluded. He's sincere all right. He thinks He's God. It's just too bad.' When people become overstrained emotionally and mentally, they get all sorts of delusions and hallucinations. A Prime Minister went to a home for mentally sick people a while ago, and chatted with the patients. He went to one man and asked his name and where he came from, and another man looked up and said, 'Excuse me, sir, who are you?' Very quietly the minister said, 'Well, I'm the Prime Minister.' 'Oh,' said the man, 'listen, don't worry about that. When I first came in here I thought I was the Pope.' 'No,' they said, 'No man in his rightful mind would say that he was God. He has a devil. He is mad.' And those who heard that, said, 'Have you heard Him preach? His are not the words of one who hath a devil. And another thing—how can a man who has a devil open the eyes of one who was born blind?'

Has the influence of Jesus of Nazareth been the influence of a deranged person? Why, of course not. As you go through the Gospels say to yourself, are these the babblings of a mad man, or are these the words of God? The chief priest and the scribes heard that the common people were saying, 'Is not this the Christ? When Christ cometh, will He do more miracles than this man doeth?' Then, said John, in the eighth chapter of his Gospel, they sent officers, the temple police to arrest Him. The soldiers made a very grave blunder. They paused for a moment on the outskirts of the crowd to listen to the preacher whom they had come to arrest, and instead of arresting the preacher, they were arrested by the preacher. An hour or so afterwards, when the benediction had been pronounced, they went back to the chief priests without the prisoner. 'Why have ye not brought Him? Where is He?' And all those simple men could say was, 'Never man spake like this man.' 'Are you also deceived?' they said. 'This people who know not the law are cursed. Certainly out of Galilee ariseth no prophet.' They did not bother to find out that Jesus did not come from Galilee, but from Bethlehem in Judaea.

I challenge you to find anything in the whole sphere of human literature to be compared with the words of Jesus. 'The words that I speak unto you,' said Jesus, 'I speak not of myself. The words that I speak unto you, they are spirit, they are life.' Said Peter, 'Lord, to whom shall we go? Thou hast the word of eternal life.'

If Jesus of Nazareth was not a bad man, if Jesus of Nazareth was not a mad man, then I submit to you that He must have been God. Those who teach, as I was taught, that Jesus was just a good man, are appallingly ignorant of the four Gospels. For if Jesus of Nazareth was not God, GOD, then He certainly was not good, GOOD, for Jesus of Nazareth said that He was God, and if He was not God, He was either mad or He was bad. The trouble with men and women of our age is we are just plain ignorant of the Bible. Because we are so ignorant of what Jesus said and what Jesus taught, all we do is to pay some lip service to Jesus of Nazareth, the prophet. I believe that there are men and women who go to church regularly, who have been baptized and confirmed, and Jesus of Nazareth, His life, death and resurrection have just as much influence on their lives as Shakespeare has upon them. No more. Why? Because they don't know or understand who He is. He demands worship, He demands that you shall give to Him every ounce of your body, every part of your mind and every emotion, and all you have, and all you are, one hundred per cent, every moment of every day. He demands it.

When the disciples came to the coast of Caesarea Philippi with Jesus, He put a question to them. Do you remember? 'Whom say men that I am?' I am always amazed at the reply they gave. They wanted to spare their master's feelings, so they said nothing about the people that said He was a deceiver, or the people that said He was mad. But they simply said, 'Well, Rabbi, some say that you're John the Baptist, risen from the dead. King Herod takes that view. Some say that you're Elijah. Some say possibly Jeremiah, or one of the prophets.' Then unexpectedly He looked at them and said, 'But whom say ye that I am?' I'm so glad that Simon Peter didn't even pause. He didn't have to, for he knew the answer. 'We believe that thou art the Christ, the Son of the living

God.' What did Jesus say? Tut, tut, silence, no, no? No. He just looked at Simon and said, 'Yes, blessed art thou Simon, son of Jonas, for flesh and blood hath not revealed it unto thee, but my Father which is in heaven. You're quite right. I am the Messiah, I am the Son of God.' Of course, the group that took that view were in the minority. I admit that. But they knew Him best.

When a man comes to me with a tall story, and I know the man who tells me the tall story to be someone who is not quite straight in business, not quite honest, I listen quietly and I say to myself, 'Yes, Tom Rees, this is a tall story. Take it with a pinch of salt.' On the other hand, when a man comes to me whom I have got to know and love and trust, a man who is sincere and real, a living Christian, a man who has a sterling character, who has a story which strikes me as being tall, when I come to repeat it I say, 'Yes, it is so, because so-and-so told me.' The sinless life that Jesus lived brings to my mind a deep assurance that the claims that He made are acceptable. Napoleon Bonaparte, who knew men intimately, and had read the Gospel story, said of Jesus, 'I know men, and Jesus of Nazareth was no mere man.' He spoke the truth.

What of the miracles Jesus performed? Even the common people when they watched his miracles, said one to another, 'When the Christ, the Messiah, cometh will He do more miracles than this man hath done?' Others said, 'This is a prophet' Others said, 'This is the Christ.' John, who in his Gospel gives us details of seven of the great miracles of Jesus, adds a footnote at the end of his Gospel saying, 'And many other signs did Jesus in the

presence of His disciples, which are not written in this
book, but these are written that ye might believe that
Jesus is the Christ, the Son of God, and that believing, ye
might have life through His name.' What miracles He
performed! He fed multitudes with a handful of bread
and fish. He called a man back from the dead who had
been dead four days, and was stinking because of the
corruption of death. He walked on the water, and gave
Peter the power to do the same. He said to the storm
raging on the Sea of Galilee, 'Peace, be still,' and the
angry waves calmed. No wonder those in the boat wor-
shipped Him saying, 'Of a truth, thou art the Son of God.'
Jesus said that His miracles 'were works which my Father
hath given me to finish. The same works that I do bear
witness of me, of the Father himself'.

The greatest proof of the deity of Jesus of Nazareth is
that He rose again from the dead. He said, 'When ye
have lifted up the Son of man—when you've nailed Him
to the Cross, when you've crucified Him—after you have
done that, you will know that I am. You come seeking
after a sign. There shall no sign be revealed unto this
wicked and adulterous generation, except the sign of the
prophet Jonah. Even as Jonah was three days and three
nights in the belly of the fish, even so must I, the Son of
man, the Messiah, be three days and three nights in the
grave. No man takes my life from me. Thank God I have
power to lay down my life. And what is more, I have
power to take my life again. I will prove to you and show
you beyond all doubt that I am God, manifest in the
flesh in that I will rise again from the dead.' Jesus of

Nazareth did not say that He was a son of God, He did not say that He was the Son of God. He said that He was God the Son. He did not claim a vague divinity for Himself. He claimed deity.

CHAPTER EIGHT

THE POWER OF THE HOLY SPIRIT

Can an intelligent person believe in the power of the Holy Spirit? Is the Holy Spirit a power that I can have and use, or is He a person—a living, loving, intelligent person—who desires to have and to use me? Exactly who is the Holy Spirit?

The Holy Spirit is the third *Person* of the Trinity. We would not speak of God the Father, or of His Son, Jesus Christ our Lord, as 'it'. So often when church-going people speak of the third Person of the Trinity, they speak of Him as 'it'. He is a living, loving, intelligent person.

I wonder whether you have ever noticed the odd grammar Jesus used when He commissioned His disciples, or, at any rate, what seems odd until we come to think about it. He said, 'Go, preach the gospel, baptising in the name of the Father, and of the Son, and of the Holy Ghost.' Not 'names' in the plural, but 'name' in the singular, signifying quite clearly the Trinity—three in one and one in three.

A student told me that he did not believe in the Trinity. Quite naturally I said, 'Why?' 'Well,' he said, 'for the very good reason that I don't understand the Trinity, and I don't believe in anything I don't understand.' I said, 'Really? Have you got television at home?' He said, 'Yes, but what's that got to do with it?' I said, 'I just wondered whether you understood television perfectly.' 'No,' he said, 'I haven't a clue how it works. Why?' I said, 'You told me just now that you didn't believe in anything you didn't understand. You believe in television, don't you? But you don't understand it.' Obviously there are ten thousand things that we do not understand, yet we believe in them. If that is true in the physical world round about us, surely the same rule can be applied to spiritual things in the religious sphere. Undoubtedly the mystery of the Trinity is something that none of us can fully understand. But we are not always called upon to be understanders. We are called upon in Christian things to be believers.

In a limited sense each one of us is a trinity. If you were to go to your doctor and ask him the simple question, 'Please, doctor, what am I?' he, being a very busy man, would give one glance at you and say, 'Flesh and blood, lots of it.' But if you put your same question to a psychologist, he would say, 'Well, mind, grey matter.' If you go to your minister, and put the same question to him, he'll say, 'You are spirit.' Are the doctor, the psychologist and the preacher contradicting one another because they give differing answers? No, they all speak the truth. Whether you like it or dislike it, whether you believe it or disbelieve it, whether you understand it or don't understand it, you consist of body and of mind and of spirit. No doctor, no preacher, no psychologist can tell you exactly where body ends and mind begins, and where mind ends and spirit begins. The plain fact is that in a limited sense we are a trinity, consisting of three parts. I am not suggesting for one moment that God is a trinity in the same sense that we are a trinity. We consist of body and of mind and of spirit; God consists of three persons in one: God the Father, the first Person, God the Son, the second Person, God the Holy Spirit, the third Person of the Trinity. Three in one and one in three.

In the fourteenth chapter of John's Gospel, Jesus speaks of the Father, He speaks of the Spirit, He speaks of Himself. Then towards the end of the chapter He speaks of the three persons of the Trinity, using the word 'We'. Indeed, in one verse, He speaks first of the Father, 'And I will pray the Father'—the first Person—'and He shall give you another Comforter'—the third Person. '*I* will pray the Father,' says the second Person of the Trinity. If you will study the fourteenth chapter of John you will see that the Lord Jesus Christ, the second Person of the Trinity, first identifies Himself intimately with the Father. 'Ye that have seen me, have seen the Father.' And secondly, He identifies Himself intimately with the Holy Spirit. 'I will not leave you comfortless; I will come to you; because I live, ye shall live.'

Never imagine that the Holy Spirit is merely a mystical power. He is a living, loving Person. You ought to come to know Him, you ought to come to love Him; you ought to seek His friendship, His fellowship, His guidance, and His power in your life. If you do not have Him dwelling in your heart and in your life, you don't stand a chance against the world and the flesh and the devil. Your only hope is in the power of the Holy Spirit.

In the fourteenth chapter of John the Lord Jesus introduces the Holy Spirit. Their hearts were confused, because He had just told them that He was going to leave them. But He said, 'Listen, no need for your hearts to be troubled and confused, because I, the Lord Jesus, am going to pray to the Father, the first Person in heaven and He is going to give you another Comforter.' And the word that Jesus used there for 'another' does not mean another one of a different kind; it means another one of precisely the same kind.

All that the Lord Jesus was to the disciples down here on earth, the Holy Spirit of God should be to us today, if we know and love Christ, if we are real, enlightened Christian people.

The apostles were not particularly pleased to hear that some stranger was coming to take the place of their beloved Master. So the Lord Jesus went further to introduce Him. First He named Him: He said, 'His name is the Spirit of truth'. Jesus Himself was the truth, and the Holy Spirit is His Spirit—the Spirit of truth. Said the Lord Jesus, 'He is no stranger to you; you already know Him. The world does not know Him, but you know Him, you've met Him, you're acquainted with Him, He is your friend already.' Unless I'm mistaken, I can see the apostles looking at the Master and then looking at one another, as they said in their hearts, 'Of whom does the Master speak? We know Him? When did we meet Him? When did we encounter Him? We know Him already? Of whom is the Master speaking?' The Lord

Jesus said, 'His name is not only the Spirit of truth, you not only know Him, but He is living with you now. He is dwelling with you now.' 'What here, Master, in the upper room?' 'Yes, here, right now.' 'Well, whoever can it be? Hope it's not Peter. Might be John, of course.' Then the Lord Jesus tore aside all mystery, and made this wonderful statement: 'I will not leave you comfortless; I will come to you. *I*, Jesus. I am the Spirit of truth who is coming, and will be living with you. I myself am coming back.' Jesus Himself was coming back again to be with them. Not coming, as He first came, in flesh and blood, but coming back in the Person of the Holy Spirit.

A Sunday School teacher asked her class, 'Who is the Holy Spirit?' That is a question that few theologians can answer correctly, but sometimes little children have a gift of being able to put profound truths into simple language. After a moment's pause, one little kid put his hand up in the air and said, 'Please, Miss, the Holy Spirit is the other self of Jesus.' Nothing could have been nearer the truth.

When you think of the Holy Spirit, do not think of a mysterious, mystical power; think of the Lord Jesus Himself, not in flesh and blood, but in His Spirit, the Spirit of truth. 'I will not leave you comfortless,' said Jesus. 'I will come to you; I have been with you.' How wonderful! Emmanuel, 'God with us.'

Jesus said, 'He hath been with you; in the future, He shall be *in* you. I in you, you in me.' I do not know any other verse in the Bible that sums up New Testament Christianity like those words do. Listen to them again: 'I in you; you in me.' That's Christianity.

Someone asked, 'What is a Christian?' The Christian person thought for a moment, then wrote the word down on a piece of paper: C H R I S T I A N. Then he said to the questioner, 'Come and look.' He took his pencil and crossed out a letter—the letter 'A', and he said, 'Now what have you got left? Just this: CHRIST IN.' And he said, 'That is a Christian—a man who has Christ in his heart.'

St. John, in his first epistle, puts it so simply, 'This is the record'—here's the word, here's the message—'God has given to us eternal life.' Eternal life in the Bible is not human life, stretched out into the life to come. It is an entirely new quality of life. 'This,' says St. John, 'is the record, God has given to us eternal life, and this life is in God's Son.' He adds: 'He that hath the Son hath life; he that hath not the Son of God, hath not life.' And the eternal life that God offers to every man and woman, every fellow and girl, is to be found only in Christ.

It is tragically possible to be baptized, to be a member of your church, to be a regular communicant, to be a Sunday School teacher, to sing in the choir, to lead a decent life, to take part in all sorts of religious activities, to read the Bible and to pray, and still deep down not to know Jesus Christ personally, not to have the power of the Holy Spirit. It is possible to have all the outward and visible signs of Christianity, and to know nothing of the inward and spiritual grace of the power and presence of God the Holy Spirit in your life.

The Holy Spirit, and the Holy Spirit alone, can help us understand the truth of Christianity. Only by the teaching and the revelation of the Holy Spirit of God can we begin to understand the Christian doctrine.

The Bible makes it clear that to the uninitiated man or woman, to the man or woman who has never received the Holy Spirit, the whole Christian faith and the whole Christian message is foolishness. St. Paul says, 'The preaching of the Cross'—that is, the Christian message— 'is foolishness to those that are perishing. But to us which are being saved, the gospel is the power of God unto salvation.'

The reason why some do not understand the truth of the Bible is that they have never received the power of the revelation of God, the Holy Spirit. Obviously, when we approach Christianity, we must give our minds to it. There is no science anywhere that is so fascinating, so profound, so exacting, as the science of theology, which means the study of God.

I hasten to add that first and foremost Christianity is not a matter of education of the mind; first and foremost it is a matter of revelation to the soul, and it is only by the light of the Holy Spirit coming in and opening our eyes, that we see any beauty in the Lord Jesus, anything in worship, in prayer, any truth laid down in God's Holy Word.

St. Paul says: 'Eye hath not seen, nor hath ear heard, nor hath it entered into the heart, the things that God hath prepared for them that love Him.' You can't see them, you can't hear them, you can't understand them. 'But,' says St. Paul, 'God by His Spirit has revealed these things to us.' It is not a matter of seeing or hearing or learning; it is a matter or revelation by God, the Holy Spirit.

There are people who ought to get down on bended knees and pray, 'Oh God, open my blind eyes. Oh God, unstop my deaf ears. Oh God, send light into my darkened heart; Oh God, give understanding to this foolish heart and mind of mine; send the light of Thy Spirit to illuminate and to teach me.' I believe that if they prayed like that, they would hear God speaking, as Jesus spoke to the disciples of old: 'And when He, the Spirit of truth is come, He will guide you, He will lead you into all the truth. He shall take of the things that are mine, and show them unto you.'

We not only need the power of God's Spirit to give us understanding and light, we need the power of the Holy Spirit to make us the children of God, by faith in Jesus Christ.

One Monday morning in a town where I was preaching, there came a knock at the door where I was staying. 'Excuse me, Mr. Rees, but the district nurse would like to see you. Could you talk to her now?' I said, 'By all means. Ask her to come in.' A woman of about sixty years of age came in, and as soon as she entered, I saw battle in her eyes. I asked her name, and we shook hands formally. I said, 'Will you sit down?' She paused for a moment, and I thought she was going to stand up and dress me down, but then looking at the chair, she sat on the edge of it bolt upright. 'Mr. Rees, I don't usually attend the church where you were preaching last night. Indeed, it's the first time in my life I've ever been to that sort of church. Did I understand you aright last night, Mr. Rees?' 'What are you referring to?' 'Did you say that we are not all the children of God? Did you, or did

you not?' I said, 'Indeed, I did. Why?' 'How dare you
say such a thing? Of course, we're all the children of God.
God made us all, didn't He?' I said, 'Indeed He did.'
'Why then, we're all children of God.' I said, 'Nurse, He
made the rats and the mice and the pigs too; are they
our brothers and sisters?' 'You've no right to talk like
that. Have you never read your Bible, Mr. Rees?' I said,
'Yes, I have—once or twice.' 'Didn't our Lord teach us,
saying, "When ye pray say, *Our Father* which art in
heaven." ' I said, 'Yes, He did.' Then I opened my Bible
and said, 'But let's read the verse before, shall we, nurse?
So that we don't misunderstand what Jesus said.' And I
read, 'And His disciples came unto Him, saying, "Lord,
teach *us* (thy disciples) to pray." And Jesus answered
and said unto them, his disciples, "When *ye* pray, *ye*
say, Our Father." ' I turned over to the eighth chapter of
John and said, 'Now listen,' and I read the words of Jesus,
speaking to other people, intensely religious, moral
people: 'Ye are of your father the devil; the lusts of your
father will ye do. He was a murderer from the beginning,
and abode not in the truth.' 'Does that come in the
Bible?' 'Come and read for yourself.' 'I've never seen
that before.' 'Well, it's here.' She said, 'I've never heard
such talk before in all my life, that we're not all the children of God.' I said, 'Of course we're not all the children
of God; we're all the creatures of God, and in that sense
we are His children. But we only become the children of
God when we receive Christ. Let me show you what St.
John says.' I opened my Bible at the first chapter and
read these words: 'He (Jesus) came unto His own (liter-
ally His own home, His own people, His own family),

and His own received Him not. But to as many as received Him to them gave He power (the authority) to
become (something that they were not before) the sons
of God, (to be born of God).'

I said, 'Nurse, you may have been to church every
week since you were a girl,' and she told me she had,
'And you may always have kept the commandments, but
unless you have opened the door of your heart and life
and received Christ as your Saviour and Lord, you've
never yet become a child of God.'

You may be baptised, you may be confirmed, you
may be a regular communicant, you may be a moral
person, you may be orthodox; but if you have never
opened the door of your heart and received Christ, then
you are not a child of God. You have not been born of
God's Spirit, and it's the Holy Spirit of God, the third
Person of the Trinity, who moves into your heart and
into your life, and causes you to be born anew, born
from above. If for the first time in your life you look up,
and instead of looking to God as a judge before whom
you tremble and fear, from your heart you cry, 'Father,
my Father,' God looks down from heaven and says, 'My
child, my child.'

My third point is that the Holy Spirit not only en-
lightens our hearts and minds and gives us understanding, He not only makes us the children of God, but the
Holy Spirit of God sets us free from the power of sin; He
sets us free from the world, from the flesh and from the
devil.

St. Paul lets us into his own secret struggle at the end
of the seventh chapter of his letter to the Romans. He

says, 'When I would do good, evil is present with me.' I know what to do, I know what is right, but I have not the power to do it. I know what is wrong, but I have not the power to avoid it. 'O wretched man that I am,' says St. Paul. 'How am I going to find deliverance from this cursed thing called sin, that seems to drag me down and entrap me and enslave me time and time again.' There shouldn't be any break between the end of chapter 7 and the beginning of chapter 8 in Romans; it should move straight on, as St. Paul answers the question. With triumph he cries, 'Thanks be to God, for the law of the Spirit of life in Christ Jesus hath made me free from the law of sin and death.'

In this space age the biggest problem in getting a man into space or a satellite launched, is the tremendous power needed to overcome the pull of gravity. Until the missile has burst through it, there is no release, there is no orbiting.

In our hearts there is a greater and stronger downward drag than the gravity of earth. It is called in the Bible the law of sin and death. Just as you take an object and let go of it, and expect it to fall with a thud to the ground; so in spite of our religion, in spite of the punishment we sin. An expert in mental hygiene said, 'We have come to believe that every child is born into the world a potential criminal.' A scientist talking, please note. He added, 'And we have come to believe that but for the restraints of human society, every child would automatically act like a criminal.'

There is only one way of release from the power of sin. It is to be found in a Person, a wonderful Person, a

Person little known, but a Person who loves you, who grieves over you when you sin. His name is the Spirit of truth, the Holy Spirit of God. He and He alone is able to enter into our hearts and into our lives, and to break the power of sin, and set us free, gloriously free.

I know from my experience, I know from the Bible, I know it from the experience of scores of others that whatever sin has got you gripped, there is an answer in the Person of the Holy Spirit, who is able and willing to bring light and understanding, to make you a child of God, and to set you free. Before you can know anything of Him, anything of His power and deliverance, you must come as a sinner to the foot of the Cross, where the second Person of the Trinity, our Lord Jesus Christ, suffered and died. There at the foot of the Cross, you must seek forgiveness.

Some of the greatest saints, the most spirit-filled men and women that I have met, are quiet humble people, who know little of ecstasy and joy in their hearts. However, they experience day by day the peace of God by the Holy Spirit, which passes all understanding.

CHAPTER NINE

THE SECOND COMING OF CHRIST

She had not been a Christian very long. Her heart was filled with love for the Lord Jesus Christ, and she longed to introduce other people to Him. She had found Christ through the local Salvation Army, and at the mercy seat she committed her life to Him. She had her new uniform and she just could not help walking up to people and asking them lovingly and sincerely, 'Are you saved? Do you know Jesus Christ, who makes all the difference to my life?' Most people were impressed; some people laughed, of course—there always will be scoffers. And then, living in a cathedral city, she spied on the pathway coming towards her a real live bishop. There he was, gaiters, hat, apron, the lot. And immediately she said to herself, 'Well, bishops too have got souls that need to be saved. I've got to talk to him. Why not?' She ought, of course, to have said, 'My Lord,' but she didn't know that, so she went up very politely and said, 'Excuse me, sir, are you saved?' I'm not sure that we ought to stop people on the street and ask them if they are saved, but I admire her pluck and enthusiasm, and I am not going to criticise her.

It so happened that the bishop was a saint who loved the Lord Jesus, and he was a great scholar too. Most saints are not scholars, and most scholars are not saints, but this bishop was a scholar and a saint. He was not trying to be funny, he just looked at her, feeling a little confused, and said, 'My dear, the New Testament speaks about salvation in three different ways: sometimes it talks about salvation as though it were a past and accomplished fact; it talks about it in the past tense. Sometimes it talks about salvation in the present tense, as if it's something that has begun, but isn't yet complete. Sometimes it talks about salvation as something that is in the future, that has not even begun. Now, my dear, tell me, do you want to know whether I am saved, or whether I'm being saved, or do you want to know shall I be saved?'

She looked up at him with a big smile and answered by just blinking—that's all she could do.

The bishop was right, of course. When Paul wrote to the Christians in Ephesus, he wrote about salvation this way: 'By grace ye have been saved, through faith.' Note the tense. 'Ye have been saved.' It is done, it is finished. When the same apostle wrote to the Christians in Corinth, talking about people's reactions to the Gospel, he said, 'The preaching of the Christian Gospel is to them that are perishing foolishness.' He hastened to add, 'But to us which are being saved, it is the power of God.'

So it is spoken of in the past tense, 'Ye have been saved'; sometimes it is spoken of in the present tense—being saved; and sometimes the New Testament talks about salvation in the future tense. For instance, in writing to the Christians in Rome, Paul says, 'Now is our salvation nearer than when we first believed.' It is nearer now than the day we were converted to Jesus Christ. 'And unto us which look for Christ's second coming, He shall appear the second time, having done with sin unto salvation.'

So the bishop was right. Sometimes the Bible says we are saved; sometimes it says we are being saved; sometimes it says we shall be saved.

One little word occurs three times in Hebrews, chapter 9. The word is 'appear'. It occurs first in the past tense, again in the present tense and the third time in the future tense.

Verse 26 says, 'But now once, in the end of the age, Christ the Lord Jesus hath appeared in this world, to put away sin by the sacrifice of Himself.' So first and foremost—Christ hath appeared. He appeared first as a little babe, in the stable at Bethlehem, because there was no room for Him in the inn. He was conceived by the Holy Ghost, He was born of the Virgin Mary, and here in this sinful world Christ appeared. He actually came; He invaded human life and human nature.

Why did He appear in this world? The answer is given in unmistakable language: 'He hath appeared to put away sin.' That is why He came.

Before His birth, a messenger from heaven appeared to Joseph and Mary, and said, 'Thou shalt call His name Jesus. For when He comes, He shall deliver His people from their sin.' He hath appeared to put away sin. The angel foretold the purpose of His coming. When our Lord was here on earth, He told us exactly why He had come. I quote His words: 'God sent His son into the world, that the world through Him might be saved.'

Years later Paul quotes one of the slogans of the early Christians: 'This is a faithful saying, worthy of all acceptation that Christ Jesus came into the world (He appeared) to save sinners.' He hath appeared to put away sin.

When Christ was here, He set us an example, He performed miracles, He taught us wonderful things about God and the kingdom of God. But the main purpose of His appearing in this world was not as an example, not as a teacher, not as a performer of miracles; first and foremost, above everything else, He appeared in this world to put away sin. That's why He came. And when we call Him Saviour, we call Him by His name.

He hath appeared to put away sin. How? By the sacrifice of Himself. He was once offered there on the Cross to bear the sin of many. Did not He say that He had come to shed His blood for the remission of sin? 'Without the shedding of blood, there is no remission'—no putting away of sin.

Christ, the Son of God, has already appeared in this world to put away our sin by the sacrifice of Himself on the Cross. He was wounded for our transgressions, He was bruised for our iniquities, and the price of our peace was heaped up upon Him, and with His stripes we are healed. All we like sheep have gone astray; we have turned everyone to his own way, yet the Lord hath laid on Him the iniquity of us all. By His death on the Cross, we can be saved once and for all from the penalty, guilt and burden of sin.

Verse 24 tells us, 'Christ is entered into heaven itself,

now to appear in the presence of God for us.' There in glory, there in power, to intercede for us, to help us, to send to us the power and grace of His Holy Spirit, to share with us His resurrection life. In the upper room Peter boasted, 'Though all men forsake thee and deny thee, yet will not I, Lord. I will die with thee.' You remember what Jesus said to Peter? He said these odd words, 'Peter, the devil has desired to get hold of you and sift you like wheat. Peter, you're going to be dropped this very night right into the sieve of the devil, and he's going to shake you and twist you and break you and bruise you.' In the near east farmers get the grain and put it into a sieve. And they shake it. If there is a breeze blowing, then all is well; the chaff is blown away or heaped to one side and burned. The corn falls to the ground, and is gathered in. It is no use until it has been into the sieve. 'This night,' says Jesus to Peter, 'the devil is going to drop you right in his sieve, and he's going to give you the most terrible winnowing you have ever had. It's going to be unpleasant, Peter.' But Jesus adds, 'But, Peter, I have prayed for thee, that thy faith fail not. Don't worry, I'm going to be with you.'

One old saint said, 'If there's no devil, I'd like to know who carries on his business for him. He does a successful job.' I did not believe in the devil when I was converted to Christ, but I had not been converted twelve hours before I realised that I was up against an intelligent, subtle foe. After I had been a Christian some months, I found that the devil was so real and temptation was so strong, that I began to wonder whether or not my soul was saved. I imagined that if I was truly saved, I would not be tempted. What a novice I was!

I went to see a minister, a lovely saint of God. I told him my problems. He quoted texts that I did not understand. We had a prayer together, and I said 'Amen' to his prayer. Then I said goodbye to him, and just as I was going down the vicarage drive, he said, 'Goodbye, Tom, bless you. Remember, when you play cricket you can't score runs unless you're bowled at. Goodbye.' I said, 'Goodbye,' and thought, what's he talking about? When you play cricket, you can't score runs unless you're bowled at. What's that got to do with religion? Then I suddenly realised that he was talking sense. With every ball that the devil sends down the pitch, his object is to get us out, to make us sin, but the captain of our salvation, the Lord Jesus Christ, is there in the grandstand of heaven, watching and praying for us. Do we run away? Not at all. We say, 'Lord, give me grace to play a straight bat, and hit this one for six.' 'We count it all joy,' as the apostle says, 'when we fall into divers temptations,' because it gives us an opportunity to score, and to bring glory to the name of our Lord and Saviour Jesus Christ. 'The devil has desired to have you and sift you like wheat, but I have prayed for you,' said Jesus.

As sure as Jesus died on the Cross, so sure is the Lord at the right hand of the throne of God, ever pleading, ever praying.

What a lovely thing it is to say, 'Thank God, I am saved from the penalty of sin; Jesus died. Thank God, I'm being saved from the power and practice of sin; Jesus lives.' But best of all, Jesus Christ is to appear again, here on earth. His second appearing. In verse 28, it says, 'And unto them that look for Him, He shall appear the second time, without sin unto salvation.'

When the Lord Jesus Christ comes back again, we shall be saved from the very presence of this cursed thing called sin. So those of us who know and love Christ, now is our salvation nearer than we first believed. Did you believe a year ago? It is a year nearer. Did you believe six months ago? It is six months nearer. It is nearer tonight than it's ever been before. Christ is coming back again.

Some people are frightened of mentioning the second coming of Christ. It has been so abused by cranky people, by people who cannot or will not read the word of God aright, but because a great truth is abused, there is no reason why it should not be believed. Jesus said, 'Let not your heart be troubled. I go to prepare a place for you, and if I go to prepare a place for you, I will come again and receive you unto myself, that where I am, there ye may be also.' I think the angels of heaven must have been listening in when Jesus spoke those words. Some weeks later, when our Lord Jesus Christ was taken up into heaven, two of the angels were appointed to stand outside the city of Jerusalem, on the Mount of Olives, where a few moments before the disciples actually saw Him taken up from them. As they watched the cloud, says St. Luke, receive Him out of their sight, while they looked steadfastly towards heaven, two men stood by them in white apparel, which said, 'Ye men of Galilee, why stand ye gazing up into heaven? This same Jesus which is taken up from you into heaven, shall so come in like manner as ye have seen Him go into heaven.' 'If I go, I will come again,' said Jesus.

Writing to the Christians in Thessalonica, Paul says a similar thing. 'If you believe that Christ died and rose again, then believe this. Even so, those that sleep in Jesus (the saints who died trusting in Christ) will God bring with Jesus.' 'And,' says St. Paul, 'what I am saying is not my own invention. It is God's word to you through me. The Lord Himself, this same Jesus, shall descend from heaven with a shout, with the voice of the arch-angel, and the trump of God, and the dead in Christ— those saints who have died trusting Christ—shall rise. Then we which are alive and remain shall be caught up together with them in clouds, to meet the Lord in the air.' 'I will come again and receive you unto myself.' 'So,' says the apostle, 'shall we ever be with the Lord.' 'That where I am, there ye may be also,' says Jesus.

St. Paul, to those hearts that were broken, bereaved and sad, adds these lovely words, 'Wherefore, because of God's word, comfort one another with these words.'

Everything in the Bible and in the world about us points to the immediate return of our Lord and Saviour, Jesus Christ. There are people who mock. Peter tells us about them. They say, 'Where is the fulfilment of His coming? Where is it? Since our parents and grandparents fell asleep, all things have gone on just the same as they did from the beginning of creation. We have always heard this story of the coming again of Jesus Christ. Where is the promise of His coming?' Peter says, 'Of this fact they are willingly ignorant—they want to re-main ignorant of this—that by the word of God, who cannot lie, the heavens and earth were created, that by the word of God—God who prophesied judgment in the

days of Noah, and judgment came by that same word—
we may rest assured that God is not slack concerning His
promise.' The reason why God tarries, the reason why
Christ does not come, is that God is longsuffering towards
us.

Hodder Christian Paperback of the Year

GOD'S SMUGGLER

by BROTHER ANDREW *with*
JOHN *and* ELIZABETH SHERRILL

The extraordinary story of a Christian missionary who
has carried the Word of God to every Communist
country, preaching to underground worshippers and
smuggling the Bible to believers behind the Iron Curtain.

Andrew's account of his mission is a story of exuberant,
danger-charged adventure for Christ, which has become
an international bestseller.

'A book you will not want to miss.' *Catherine Marshall*

I'VE GOT TO TALK TO SOMEBODY GOD

by
MARJORIE HOLMES

It is difficult to keep up with the demand for these apron pocket prayers for women. Catherine Marshall writes: 'This book is for every woman, every day.'

THE LIVING NEW TESTAMENT

paraphrased by
KENNETH TAYLOR

The New Testament in everyday language—for everyone. Few other modern translations have so caught the interest of young and old alike.

'I read with renewed interest and inspiration the age-abiding truths of the New Testament as though they had come direct to me from God.' *Dr Billy Graham*